MERRITT LIBRARY

945.07 CO
Connor, J
The last
Michelangelo and the

D0389554

THE LAST JUDGMENT

THE LAST JUDGMENT

MICHELANGELO AND THE DEATH OF THE RENAISSANCE

James A. Connor

palgrave
macmillan

Thompson-Nicola Regional District
Library System
300-465 VICTORIA STREET
KAMLOOPS, BC   V2C 2A9

THE LAST JUDGMENT

Copyright © James A. Connor, 2009.

All rights reserved.

First published in 2009 by
PALGRAVE MACMILLAN®
in the United States—a division of St. Martin's Press LLC,
175 Fifth Avenue, New York, NY 10010.

Where this book is distributed in the UK, Europe and the rest of the
world, this is by Palgrave Macmillan, a division of Macmillan Publishers
Limited, registered in England, company number 785998, of Houndmills,
Basingstoke, Hampshire RG21 6XS.

Palgrave Macmillan is the global academic imprint of the above companies and has companies and representatives throughout the world.

Palgrave® and Macmillan® are registered trademarks in the United States,
the United Kingdom, Europe and other countries.

ISBN: 978–0–230–60573–2

Library of Congress Cataloging-in-Publication Data is available from the
Library of Congress.

A catalogue record of the book is available from the British Library.

Design by Newgen Imaging Systems (P) Ltd., Chennai, India.

First edition: July 2009

10 9 8 7 6 5 4 3 2 1

Printed in the United States of America.

1018521514

CONTENTS

ACKNOWLEDGMENTS

Among the living, I would like to thank my editor Alessandra Bastagli and her assistant Colleen Lawrie. They are the best editorial team I have ever encountered. Sometimes, they had to whack me like a stubborn mule, but the book was all the better for it. I would also like to thank my agent Giles Anderson, for being a steady rock of ages. Also, my wife Beth; without her ministrations, I couldn't find my shoes. Finally, my mother Marguerette Woods Connor, who passed on the faith, both in art and religion.

Among the dead, I would like to thank my father John Connor and Beth's father William Craven, for their unstinting support, both in this world and in the next. Flannery O'Connor, whose literary riffs have driven me forward, and Michelangelo Buonarroti, whose divine madness transformed my life.

PROLOGUE:
STANDING IN THE SISTINE

*I*t was August and Rome was sticky hot. We had made the mistake of walking up the Tiber from Trastevere toward the Vatican, so by the time we arrived, we were sweaty and uncomfortable. The area along the Tiber smelled mildly of urine, and everyone we passed looked frazzled, even the long-time Romans. We wanted to see the Sistine Chapel because we had heard so much about it and about the famous ceiling, and, more to the point, we had seen Charlton Heston play Michelangelo in the movie. The way to the Sistine Chapel was through the Vatican Museum, at the end of the long tour past the Caravaggios, the Titians, the papal portraits by Sebastiano del Piombo, the statue of Romulus and Remus being suckled by a she-wolf, the busts of Livia and Claudius, of Tiberius and Nero. And there was never any place to sit down. It was as if they didn't want you to stay and linger over the art. You were compelled to keep moving, on to the Sistine Chapel and then back out to the hot street.

The problem with the Sistine Chapel is that the place is so astounding and the trek to get there is so long, that no one wants to leave. The room fills quickly with tourists, and the line into the chapel backs up like cars on an interstate. After the long haul through the museum, I was ready to find a side door and duck out. But there were no side doors except the ones leading to the Vatican Gardens, and the Swiss

Guards were standing around there looking like cops. Once inside, most of the people clustered in the middle, craning their necks to see the famous ceiling. That was why I had come, and I joined them. I was a little disappointed because the ceiling was very high and I couldn't see much of the detail. Sidling up to tour guides who pointed out the various panels, I squinted and peered like everyone else until my neck began to hurt.

After a few minutes, tired of peering, I looked for my wife to grouse at her about the heat and about my aching feet, and to ask her to follow me out of the chapel onto the street where we could get a glass of water or maybe a beer. As I turned to find her in the crowd, my eye caught the altar wall and stuck there, at Michelangelo's other great Sistine fresco, the *Last Judgment.* Unlike the ceiling, which unfolds the long story of salvation history spun out over thousands of years, the *Last Judgment* captures a single instant, stop-time as in a photograph, a mad swirling drama like storm clouds caught in the act, a fresco full of *terribilità,* the catastrophe at the end of time. It was angst to the point of fury.

Terribilità is the term that his contemporaries used to describe Michelangelo's personality as well. It was an apt description, for Michelangelo was the first great Romantic hero, hounded by guilt, grumpy, easily wounded, brooding, fretful, fearful, raging. Probably a homosexual at a time when even the accusation of sodomy could get you executed, he likely lived a chaste life, beset by the kind of free-floating guilt that only Catholicism can generate. The *Last Judgment* was Michelangelo's most direct expression of the terror at the bottom of his psyche. The fresco, newly restored to the bright colors that Michelangelo intended, drew me in and I stood transfixed. For the first time that day, I forgot how hot it was and how much my feet hurt.

The effect of the entire fresco is like a cyclone—with the dead rising in the lower section on Christ's right side, launching themselves heavenward like Atlas rockets, swirling over the top, and the damned battling angels and demons alike on Christ's left hand, sinking violently to the River Styx and the boat of Charon, who ferries the damned to eternal punishment. Here was Dante mixed with Savonarola, a vision of the end of the world as disastrous as atomic war, exploding in the sky with Christ as the judge.

Michelangelo's fresco depicted a last judgment unlike any other that I had seen. This was a common theme for artists around Rome and, indeed, throughout Italy and Germany, especially after the fourteenth century and the Black Death. Judgment scenes are intensely cosmological, summing up creation in one big bang. But in the other examples that I had seen, the end of the world was also stately, frozen, and hierarchical. Christ appeared at the top of every fresco, with the saints and angels directly below him, the souls in purgatory below them, and the damned at the bottom, often being jeered at by demons. These paintings almost always depicted a medieval universe, a biblical flat earth with the firmament of heaven stretched over the top, and the empyrean, full of divine fire, over that. Evil was down and good was up. The rest was simply a matter of putting people in their proper stations in between. The poor of the earth, the martyrs and the prophets, the suffering and the repentant sinners were first and those who had once been first—the kings, the barons, the lords, and yes, even the popes—would be last.

But this was not the design of Michelangelo's *Last Judgment*. Here, Christ is at the dramatic center of the fresco, so that souls rising from the earth and sinking back down swirl about him and over his head. The static design of other last judgments had given way to a terrifying dynamism, full of tension and anxiety. Even the elect look to Christ, fearful of their own status in the kingdom of God. The damned, of course, show nothing but terror, eyes wide with fear of the place that awaits them. "And who shall abide on the day of his coming," said Isaiah the prophet, "and who shall stand when he appeareth?"

And what a different Christ this was! Unlike the immobile, conventionally bearded Christ of Byzantine and Medieval iconography, this Christ rises from his seat in anger, determined in the act of condemnation. He is depicted as a young Apollo, beardless and with curly hair, surrounded by a golden aureole as if lit by the sun itself.

He seems to be rising from a throne and commencing the great catastrophe with a gesture. By his presence and by his action all things are set into motion. He is naked, or nearly so, which you would expect at the end of the world—there is not much room for fashion in either heaven or hell. But this Christ is more than just naked. He is titanic and muscular like a Greek god, as one who is ready for war. His arms are spread in opposite directions, his right hand raised in condemnation of the damned. His gesture evokes Scripture: "Depart from me you cursed into the everlasting fire prepared for Satan and his angels." His left hand points to the wound on his side to show the elect the source of their salvation. His face is turned away, not necessarily toward the blessed but in rejection of the damned, the evil ones. The Virgin is no longer kneeling before him in intercession but now clings to him, her eyes turned away from the damned in pity and horror. The time for her influence is over—now is the time of judgment.

Around him, on the left and right are the martyrs holding out the symbols of their suffering and of their offices. Saint Peter holds out to Christ the keys of the kingdom. Saint Bartholomew holds out his flayed skin with its sagging face into which Michelangelo painted his own features. Saint Sebastian holds a handful of arrows; Saint Lawrence holds the grille on which he was roasted. Above on both sides, the angels seem caught in the cyclone and tumble about. Over and to the right of the place where the dead are rising, angels blow trumpets to call them forth. Beneath them, the dead are rising from their graves, some as complete bodies and some as mere skeletons. Those with eyes climb out of their graves stunned, as if seeing the truth of things for the first time. In the background, two of the elect launch themselves into the sky like missiles, determined to find a place among the angels.

Interestingly, the cosmological proclamation of the fresco looks like a sun-centered universe. Christ as Apollo is at the dramatic center, with the elect, the saints and angels, martyrs, and the damned all swirling around him like planets, or asteroids. This seemed strange to me. As a historian of science, I expected the sixteenth-century universe to be Ptolemaic, that is, geocentric. But here it looked as if Michelangelo painted a sun-centered cosmos before Copernicus published his book *On the Revolutions of Celestial Spheres.* Leonardo da Vinci wasn't the only Renaissance painter to encode ideas of the time into his work. In fact, it was a common practice. Most of these encoded ideas were theological, for what is a Renaissance fresco if not frozen theology? And last judgments especially so.

The Catholic Church was generally opposed to Copernicus, who delayed publication of his work until September 1543 for fear of condemnation. And yet two popes, Clement VII and Paul III, the latter who established the Jesuits, commissioned Michelangelo to paint the *Last Judgment,* its encoded secrets intact. Both popes knew what was there, hidden in the swirl of resurrected bodies. Later generations hardly noticed this cosmology and condemned him more for his nudes than his cosmos. Official condemnation of Copernicus would have to wait until Galileo a century later.

There is no indication that Galileo knew about what lay hidden in the *Last Judgment.* Nor is there any indication that Michelangelo knew that what he was painting would herald the modern world. Realizing this, as I stood in the middle of the Sistine Chapel, staring at the *Last Judgment* over the heads of jostling tourists who were squinting at the more famous ceiling, I felt that I was holding on to a great secret. A heavyset German man with thick glasses tripped and fell into me. "*Entschuldigen Sie,*" he said, his eyes still locked onto the fresco above.

Working my way through the crowd, I squeezed toward the altar wall of the chapel. A cluster of tourists stood there, near a Swiss guard in full Renaissance uniform, designed by Michelangelo. I felt oddly uncomfortable standing before the wall, in that select group of bystanders. Outside the chapel, the world raged on, but like most of those around me, I was drawn into the fresco, until

I had to ask myself the one inevitable question, the question that obsessed Michelangelo as he painted the fresco: Where will I be in this scene?

I thought about this, brooded over it all the way out to the street, where my wife and I huddled under an umbrella at a gelato stand a hundred feet from St. Peter's Square. A 757 rumbled overhead toward Leonardo da Vinci airport. I was back in the modern world, and the earth was spinning under my feet.

INTRODUCTION

The Dying Pope

$\mathcal{I}$n 1490, a fiery Dominican priest, Girolamo Savonarola, returned to Florence and took up the post of master of studies at the monastery of San Marco. Originally from Ferrara, he had been stationed in Florence in 1482, but the people laughed at his accent, calling him an ungainly and weak orator. He left Florence in 1487 and moved to Bologna, where he worked hard on his oratorical skills, so that when he returned to Florence in 1490 his passionate sermons at Mass on Sundays made everyone in the city sit up straight and pay attention.

Savonarola told the people truths that they would be wary to speak even to themselves, condemning the corruption of the popes, cardinals, and bishops, calling them bad shepherds who would be the first to find the flames of hell.[1] Then he carried his condemnations one step further by excoriating the rich and powerful, accusing even Lorenzo de Medici, Lorenzo the Magnificent, of usury, corruption, and tyranny.[2] The Medici had once been middle-class wool merchants in Florence, though they eventually grew rich in the banking trade. This made them morally suspect since according to Savonarola, it was a sin to lend money at interest. The denunciation of banking was not a new idea, for Savonarola was merely following a moral doctrine that had been part of Church as far back as the Middle Ages.[3]

Savonarola was one of the first great church reformers. Predating even Luther, he was an early proponent of republicanism and an implacable enemy of dictatorship.[4] He wanted to see Florence free of Medici rule and of aristocrats in general because he believed that power and wealth destroyed the Christian vision of life, and his ideas for a reform of government were an integral part of his desires for reform of the church. He also targeted the papacy in his excoriations—the pope in 1490 was Innocent VIII, who was reputed to have sold church offices to the highest bidder. In 1492, the notorious Alexander VI Borgia, who was known as a murderer and a whoremonger—and was unashamed of it all—succeeded Innocent as pope. It was said that he was proud of his sexual virility and exercised it as often as he could, and in the end produced at least eight children.[5] Even today he is listed among the "bad popes," those who by their behavior have shamed the papacy in a particularly scandalous way.[6] Savonarola, on the other hand, was an ascetic, a man who sought to live a truly Christian life, and when people mentioned that he was up against the political powerhouse of Alexander VI, he would say sarcastically, "Ah! Poor little friar!"[7] The problem with Savonarola was that he wanted everyone else to be as ascetic as he was, and he vehemently preached against the immorality of the Florentines. "This city shall no more be called Florence, but a den of thieves, of turpitude, and bloodshed."[8] He was wildly courageous and was never afraid to speak his mind or to tell powerful people what he thought of their power.

Savonarola arrived in Florence by foot, brought there at the invitation of Lorenzo de Medici, on the advice of Count Pico della Mirandola, a famous Neo-Platonic philosopher. The passionate Dominican was on fire with reform, inspiring a young man called Michelangelo Buonarroti with his zeal. On Sundays, Michelangelo would walk from the Medici palace to join the crowds at San Marco to attend Savonarola's masses. He was struck by the preacher's style and erudition, his overflowing passion, and his hunger for righteousness. A good Catholic boy, Michelangelo even considered becoming a friar in Savonarola's community, and although that never happened, he always agreed with the reformer on three issues: the naked corruption of the hierarchy, the love of power of the aristocracy, and the belief in rule by the people.

As the Medici family gradually swept away the remnants of the old Florentine republic, established in the tenth century, and set themselves in its place as Renaissance princes, Savonarola saw in them the devil's hand. He prepared a series of incandescent Lenten sermons, preached on Sundays during the six weeks of Lent, full of apocalyptic imagery. As the Lenten Season led up to Good Friday and Easter Sunday, he called the congregation to a deeper repentance. His regular topics included the evils of bishops and popes, the oppression of the poor by the rich, and the injustices perpetrated by the Medici, often calling to mind the lurid fate of sinners at the Last Judgment. Later, toward the end of 1490, he preached another eighteen sermons during the four weeks of Advent, the season leading up to Christmas. These drew such crowds that Savonarola's career as a prophet and reformer was cemented. In one of his Advent sermons, he ridiculed the practice of sending a second or third son off to the clergy.

> Fathers make sacrifices to this false idol, urging their sons to enter the ecclesiastical life, in order to obtain benefices and prebends; and thus you hear it said: *Blessed the house that owns a fat curé.*[9]

Like Jesus, Savonarola cleansed the temple with a rod, believing that corrupt clergymen were beyond salvation in that they had abandoned their flocks to the wolves. We can only speculate how this affected the young Michelangelo, with the reformer's passion resonating in his head and stirring his own yearning for righteousness. Then Savonarola set his rod upon the state, only one step below the corrupt church, where the princes and their courts used their offices only to gather more power. All of Florence could understand his message for they had only recently lost their republic to the maneuvering of the Medici.

When Lorenzo became ill and took to his bed in 1492, he called his servants to him and gave orders to complete his worldly affairs. He then sent for Savonarola, whom he admired, even though the preacher had railed against him and his family.[10] He asked for the sacrament

of Penance, and Savonarola agreed on three conditions. First, he had
to make amends to those he harmed; second, he had to give back all
his wealth accumulated through usury, or at least to command his
son to do so. Lorenzo agreed with both of these demands. And third,
Lorenzo had to give Florence its freedom and stop his family's rule
over the city. At that, according to his biographers, Lorenzo turned his
face to the wall, for he could not agree.[11]

When Lorenzo died in April 1492, Florentine life changed. With
the ascension of Lorenzo's incompetent son Piero, Savonarola had his
chance to create the Christian republic he longed for. After Piero took
his father's place as ruler of Florence, he immediately tried to rid himself of the meddlesome Savonarola, who was leading the opposition
to his family's rule. He pressured Savonarola's Dominican superiors
to remove him from Florence for a while, and to send him back to
Bologna.

During his time in Bologna, from February to April 1493,
Savonarola preached a series of Lenten sermons that shook that city.
Ginevra Bentivoglio, the wife of the lord of Bologna, often came
late to mass, leading her noisy entourage up the aisle during the sermon. After mass, he spoke quietly with her, and requested that she
appear at mass on time. Miffed by his admonishment, she returned
the next Sunday making more noise than ever. He pointed a finger
at her and shouted, "You see? Here is the Devil, coming to interrupt
God's word!"[12] Furious, the lady commanded her grooms to assassinate Savonarola while he was still preaching, but for fear of sacrilege
they refused.

The following year, Charles VIII of France gathered an army of
25,000 men with 8,000 Swiss mercenaries and entered Italy through
Genoa. Because of France's previous conquests in Italy, Charles
claimed the throne of the kingdom of Naples, which was ruled
by the Spanish at the time. After conquering Milan, he marched
through Tuscany toward Naples, pillaging along the way. Following
Florentine tradition, Piero attempted to remain neutral. This irritated the king of France, who immediately turned and marched on
Florence.

Before the French arrived, Savonarola returned to Florence, and preached a sermon on September 21, 1494 that predicted in lurid terms the impending destruction of the city. The people had no problems believing this prophecy because they knew that the French king was besieging Pisa, and was almost on their doorstep. This sermon had such apocalyptic power that it made Count Pico della Mirandola's hair stand on end. Della Mirandola had been an early proponent of Savonarola's reforms, and had no doubts about the veracity of the friar's predictions. Michelangelo was present for that sermon and it frightened him so much that he fled the city in a panic, certain that the end had come.

With Charles on the way, Piero de Medici tried to raise an army to defend the city, but because they were under the influence of Savonarola, the Florentines refused to cooperate. When Piero saw the size of the French army besieging Pisa, he opened negotiations with them and capitulated immediately, handing over two important client states. Florence erupted over Piero's failure and mobs looted the Palazzo de Medici, driving the family into exile in Bologna and reinstituting the Florentine Republic.

Taking advantage of the power vacuum, Savonarola stepped into the breach and became one of the leaders of the revolutionary movement, following his lead, the Florentine *Signoria*—the city's ruling body—accepted all but his most radical proposals. He was the man of the moment. This did not sit well with the Borgia pope, Alexander VI; he could not tolerate that a simple monk could hold such power. Moreover, it annoyed him that Savonarola had criticized the clergy and the aristocracy with such force that he had successfully roused a city to rebellion.

In 1494, just after the expulsion of the Medici and the return of the republic, Michelangelo, fearing that Savonarola might target him because of his nude sculptures and his association with the Medici, left Florence for Bologna. In Bologna, he was able to ride out the storm that was breaking in his native city while still catching all the news. He stayed in the house of Gianfrancesco Aldrovandi, a lover of Florentine culture. Aldrovandi made Michelangelo read from Petrarch and Dante every night before he fell asleep, and the two men discussed Florence's greatest poet for hours until Michelangelo became an expert on the

Divine Comedy. This background in the work of Petrarch and Dante would play a significant role in the painting of the *Last Judgment.*

Back in Florence, Savonarola's attacks grew increasingly political, undermining the already unstable slippery relationship between secular and religious authority. The pope sent one bull of censure after another, but Savonarola ignored them. In 1497, the friar and his followers staged the bonfire of the vanities by sending boys, those he called "his children," to all the houses in the city, pressuring the people to gather their worldly possessions—mirrors, musical instruments, fine clothes, fancy adornments, gambling items—and throw them into the fire. Thus the world would be purged of the instruments of sin. Meanwhile, the flames of Savonarola's rhetoric set fire to the city once again. He prophesied doom for the church and referred to himself as a prophet of God, a Jeremiah warning the people of the coming conflagration.

Alexander VI had had enough. On May 13, 1497, he excommunicated Savonarola, accusing him of heresy, prophecy, uttering sedition, and other dogmatic shenanigans. This time, the pope's censure took effect, because the citizens of Florence had become weary of the friar's preaching and were grumbling against his strictures. He had outlawed gambling, blasphemy, drunkenness, lewd conduct, adultery, and had changed the punishment for sodomy from a fine to death by burning. Some of the most prominent homosexual men had fled the city in fear to live in exile in Rome. For over a year, the street gamblers had scattered when the "children of Savonarola" appeared, but by 1497, just before the second Bonfire of the Vanities, the children were beaten as they gathered worldly objects to burn.[13] The Medici quickly returned to power through a coup d'état supported by the pope, who in 1498 demanded that they arrest and execute Savonarola. The Medici and their supporters, bereft of the even-handed leadership of Lorenzo, were happy to oblige; the government arrested Savonarola. He was bound by the wrists and left suspended from a beam until the bindings cut deeply into his wrists, a method of torture called *il strappado.*

Eventually, Savonarola confessed to plotting to kill the pope. The new Medici government tried him and hanged him in the Piazza della Signoria as crowds who once adored him screamed their bile at him, and then burned his body while it was still on the scaffold. But the city never forgot him. Michelangelo had been living in Rome at the time, at work carving the *Bacchus,* a statue of the Roman god of wine for Cardinal Riario, and the famous Roman *Pietà,* where an outsized Blessed Virgin holds the body of the crucified Jesus, for the French cardinal Jean de Billheres. He returned to Florence in time to see Savonarola's execution, an experience that haunted him for the rest of his life.

When Savonarola's denouncer, Alexander VI, finally died in 1505, his body was left untended for so long that it swelled like a balloon with postmortem gases and the papal attendants had to squeeze it into his coffin. The Roman people saw this as a punishment from God. Julius II was elected soon after. His birth name was Giuliano della Rovere, the nephew of Pope Sixtus IV, and he was the pope who commissioned the Sistine Chapel. His nickname was *Il Papa Terrible,* because of his fiery temper and his militant foreign policy.

When Alexander's successor, Pope Julius, died Rome wept. People from all over Europe trekked to the city to give homage to the warrior pope and to sneak a peek at the ceiling of the Sistine Chapel. Here Michelangelo's masterwork, commissioned by Julius, ensured that the two men, pope and painter, would be engraved into the common memory of Christendom.

The beloved Julius was succeeded by a Medici pope, Leo X. In 1520, when he excommunicated Martin Luther, the trumpet of reform soon became the trumpet of revolt. When Leo died the following year, the Catholic Church found itself in the vacillating hands of his cousin, the Medici pope Clement VII. Some historians have called him "the disastrous pope," for his decisions all too often went badly. Clement was the illegitimate son of Lorenzo de Medici's martyred brother Giuliano, who was assassinated during the *Pazzi* uprising in April 1478. During the Pazzi uprising, rivals of the Medicis, with the support of Pope Alexander VI, attacked Lorenzo and his brother during mass on Sunday, leaving Giuliano dead. The rebellion was quickly put down, and the conspirators executed and their families banished.

Clement's election to the papacy had been close. Had it not been for Emperor Charles V's political maneuvering during the conclave, he would never have ascended the papal throne. Charles was a Hapsburg, and a true believer in his divinely given right to rule. He could lay claim to Spain, Austria, Germany, Bohemia (the modern Czech Republic), and Moldavia. The problem was that since he had ensured Clement's election, Charles expected that Clement would forever be his man and would follow imperial policy, especially when that policy would lead him into war with France. For the protection of Italy, however, Clement engaged the church in the League of Cognac, a group of nations opposed to the Hapsburg Empire. The current heart of that empire was Spain, which had been enriched by gold from the New World. Charles V, the Holy Roman Emperor had claimed the Kingdom of Naples, largely because of earlier Spanish conquests as the kings of France and the Holy Roman Emperors seesawed across the Italian peninsula. Charles V wanted to unite all of Italy under his banner, and he was seeking to extend his power throughout the peninsula and from there to dominate Europe. He had convinced himself that to protect Christendom from the Turks, and to purge Christendom of Protestants, he needed to conquer all of Italy. The League of Cognac, which included England, France, Venice, Milan, and Clement VII, disagreed with Charles and sought to keep that from happening. The league selected the Duke of Urbino, Francesco Maria della Rovere, a nephew of Pope Julius, to lead their armies against the emperor's forces but he was a disaster. The Duke's caution, along with his hatred of the Medici got the better of him, and instead of attacking the Emperor's army, he set up camp, delaying action until the opportunity to attack was lost, leaving the pope and Rome exposed.

This led to the terrible events of 1527, when Charles V's army shook Rome like a dog shaking a rabbit. Michelangelo was in Rome as the emperor's army pillaged its way toward the city. He could see which way events would fall even if Clement couldn't, so he snuck out of the city and fled to Florence before the imperial army arrived.

The Imperial army had entered Italy with only promises of pay, without guarantees of food or clothing. After they defeated the French army, they expected to be paid, but once again, the emperor could not find the money. The entire army of 34,000 soldiers mutinied, and at gunpoint, forced their commander, Charles III, Duke of Bourbon, to march on Rome. The Duke was also the Constable of France, the empire's sworn enemy, but he had quarreled with the French king, Francis I because the king would not pay the money he owed the Duke, and so the Duke ended up in the employment of the emperor as a mercenary. Apart from some 6,000 Spaniards under the Duke, the army included some 14,000 *Landsknechts*, or mercenary lancers, under Georg von Frundsberg, a radical Lutheran who wanted to bring down the papacy, a small contingent of Italian infantrymen led by Fabrizio Maramaldo, Sciarra Colonna, and Luigi Gonzaga, and a cavalry regiment under Ferdinando Gonzaga and Philibert, Prince of Orange. The emperor's goal was to undermine the temporal power of the pope. Many of his Protestant soldiers wanted to hang Clement and destroy the papacy for religious reasons, but Luther would have nothing to do with the idea. Still, the real reason that the soldiers— German, Spanish, and Italian—wanted to invade Rome was to hunt for gold. Avarice had made them less of an army and more of a pack of wolves.

The Duke left Arezzo on April 20, 1527. His undisciplined troops sacked Acquapendente and San Lorenzo alle Grotte, and occupied Viterbo and Ronciglione, reaching the walls of Rome on May 5. Charles had purposely sent the troops into Italy to starve, in order to turn them into a raving mob that would then set upon the city of Rome and tear it apart. The emperor didn't particularly care how many of them died—he had killed some 100,000 troops in his war to conquer the Netherlands.

By the time the imperial army reached Rome in May 1527, the German soldiers had become ghosts of men, and all they cared about was food, wine, women, and gold. The emperor's army attacked Rome from the west, between the walls of the Vatican and the Janiculum hill, just south of the walls. There were only 5,000 defenders of Rome, but they could field a respectable artillery, something the emperor's army could not do. When the Germans began to storm the walls of the city, the imperial generals had all died or become incapacitated.

One of the eyewitness accounts we have of the battle was from the goldsmith and sculptor Benvenuto Cellini.[14] Cellini worked for Pope Clement and wrote an autobiography about his experiences during the Sack of Rome. He claimed to have shot the arquebus ball that killed the Duke of Bourbon, while he was encouraging his men onward, climbing a ladder to the top of the wall. The only man left in charge of the troops was the inexperienced Philibert, Prince of Orange, and he could not control the mob that had become his army. They quickly breached the walls of Rome and spread through the city like army ants. The pope's general, Renzo da Ceri, refused to destroy the bridges leading into the Vatican because he overestimated his ability to protect the city and underestimated the fury of the Emperor's army, and because he thought that it would lower the morale of the people. Also, he feared that the houses in Trastevere, just south of the Vatican and on the same side of the Tiber, would fall into the river if the bridges were destroyed. He had assured Clement that he could defend the city, but soon after the walls had been breached, the people in the city found him running for his life.

The pope himself had only barely escaped. As the soldiers entered the city, he was in the Sistine Chapel praying fervently. His attendants dragged him out of the chapel to see that the enemy had arrived, breaking through at Santo Spirito and coming toward him like a tide. Had he lingered in the papal apartments any longer, he would have been taken prisoner in his own palace. They surely would have hanged him if they didn't torture him to death first. The pope arrived at Castel Sant'Angelo, the papal fortress in Rome, just as its doors were closing.

The German soldiers appeared soon after and stood at the gate calling for Clement to come down so they could hang him.

According to medieval rules of warfare, the sacking of a city should last only three days. After three days, the Prince of Orange sent riders out among the men to tell them that the time had passed and that the sack had ended. The soldiers ignored the messengers and continued to rape and loot. Three days passed, then five, then ten. Then six months had passed. All throughout the city the common people screamed and cried like the damned. Every woman caught by the soldiers was raped. Young girls were raped in front of their parents, and their fathers forced to help. Meanwhile, the Spanish held everyone, rich or poor, for ransom, and those who could not pay were tortured to death. Sometimes, they even tortured those whose families could pay.

The *Landsknecht* killed every priest they could find, surrounding them and forcing them to eat feces and to drink urine as a mockery of the sacred bread and wine. They looted every monastery, every church, and every convent they could find, hauling the nuns out and raping them. They extorted money, tossed infants out of windows and laughed as they splattered on the streets while their mothers watched, forced the mothers to have sex with pigs or to run through the streets naked, and then forced the women to climb into latrines to look for hastily buried treasures.

All this time, Pope Clement and his court watched the wasting of their city from the walls of Castel Sant'Angelo, helpless. Clement knew that it was partly his own miscalculation that had brought the city to this. He had refused to take the threats of the emperor's army seriously and had trusted what Renzo da Ceri had told him about Rome's defense. Clement had been convinced that the army of the League of Cognac under Francesco Maria della Rovere would appear before the imperial army attacked.

One could not walk the streets without seeing dead bodies decomposing where they had fallen. The soldiers didn't bother to burn the dead, so plague invaded the city as well, trapping those citizens and soldiers alike who were left standing. Meanwhile, the Prince of Orange settled himself in the pope's apartments and, not wanting his horses to be stolen by his own men, stabled the animals in the Sistine Chapel. On June 6, 1527, Clement VII surrendered, and agreed to pay a ransom of 400,000 ducati in exchange for his life, though the imperial troops kept him imprisoned in the fortress for another three months.[15]

Hearing that Clement VII was safely imprisoned in the Castel Sant'Angelo, the Florentines rose up against the Medici clan once again, breaking with the pope, who was its senior member. The new government appointed Michelangelo to join the Nine of War, the war council, and instructed him to take over the construction of the city defenses. In June 1528, envoys of the pope and emperor signed the Peace of Barcelona. The pope promised to meet the emperor in Bologna and to crown him Holy Roman Emperor, just as Charlemagne had been. The emperor agreed to restore the Medici to power in Florence.

The Prince of Orange surrounded Florence and Michelangelo successfully led the defense of one of the strong points on a hill overlooking the city, San Miniato del Monte, where he had fortified the bell tower with bales of wool to cushion artillery fire. With help from Charles V—the same emperor who had released his soldiers to sack Rome, to rape and extort their way through the city but who was now an ally—Clement cut off supplies to Florence and starved its people until plague broke out. Michelangelo's favorite brother, Buonarroto, died in that 1528 plague while Michelangelo held him in his arms. Meanwhile, Florence's *condottiere,* the military commander, Malatesta Baglioni had been negotiating on the side with the imperial troops, and ceased his defense of the city, so that the Florentine republicans were forced to sue for peace.

Florence had resisted imperial power for eleven months, but finally on August 10, 1530, the city fell. As part of the city's surrender, Clement made promises of amnesty for the rebels, though he didn't intend to keep them. Instead, he sent Francesco Guicciardini, a Florentine historian and diplomat who detested the Medici but worked for them nonetheless, to root out the leaders of the rebellion in Florence and to hang them. Michelangelo went into hiding while the pope took savage vengeance on the city, his soldiers torturing and hanging the leaders, stripping others of their fortunes and sending them into the night as beggars. Baglioni sent one priest who had preached against the Medici during the siege to Clement in Rome, where the pope threw him into a dungeon at the bottom of Castel Sant'Angelo and starved him to death by slowly decreasing his rations.

In 1534, two days before the pope died, Michelangelo arrived in Rome. Attendants rushed him into the papal apartment, where Clement VII lay propped up on his deathbed, surrounded by cardinals, chamberlains, secretaries, and servants. Clement was the last of the Medici popes and probably the most hated man in Rome. Described as a cold fish by some, he was probably just shy—an introvert who saw so many sides of a question that he was frozen into indecision. He was also an accomplished self-deceiver. He could be cruel and vindictive, but he could also be thoughtful, take delight in new ideas, and be carried away by the Renaissance passion for beauty. He had plenty of money, a drive to build great things, and a desire to support artists wherever he found them.

Michelangelo had known Pope Clement longer than any of his other patrons, because the two of them had grown up together in the house of Lorenzo the Magnificent. At fifty-eight years old, the pope's favorite artist was the same pugnacious man he had been in his twenties, though time and strife had softened his edges. When he was painting the Sistine Chapel ceiling, Michelangelo had locked himself into the chapel and refused to let his own assistants in. He went grumpily around town in a crushed felt hat when he was working, and he was always working. He laughed easily, however, a quality that had grown in him over the years, and felt passionately—Clement knew that with Michelangelo, a soft word always worked better than a stick, because his favorite artist had a short fuse and rarely forgave an insult. Back in Florence, when Michelangelo was a young man, Leonardo da Vinci had snubbed him, and in retaliation, he turned on the man and ridiculed him about the great bronze horse he had built for the Sforza family in Milan. The two were only politely cordial with each other after that.

Unlike Leonardo, who sometimes dabbled and often left projects half done, Michelangelo's own art consumed him, oppressed him, and was a crucial outlet for his fierce energies. Of average height, with a broken nose that looked as if it had been squashed into his face, Michelangelo was, even as he neared sixty, still muscular from long days with the hammer and chisel. He was perpetually vigilant about his honor, insults (real and imagined), and money. His one constant gripe with his family in Florence—his father Ludovico and his brothers Buonarroto, Giovansimone, and Gismondo—was about the money he sent them and what they did with it. In letter after letter, he complained bitterly about the hardness of his life and the suffering he endured for their sake, and how little they appreciated him.

The day in 1534 that Michelangelo arrived in the papal apartment, he found his childhood friend, who had once been handsome and thoughtful, now shriveled with disease. Clement was nearly blind, jaundiced, and twisted with intestinal pain. As his death approached, rumors about plots and intrigues flew around Rome like pigeons. Rumor had it that the pope had been poisoned either by an agent of the French king, Francis I, or by an agent of the Holy Roman Emperor Charles V, both of whom hated him because he had refused to firmly take either of their sides in the endless struggles between the French and the Spanish. The goldsmith Benvenuto Cellini, who was then in the service of Pope Clement, had visited Clement the day before. Cellini later wrote in his autobiography that the poor man was so blind, even though he called for his spectacles and for a candle, he could not see the engraving on the medallions Cellini had brought him and could only rub his thumb over the gold metal and sigh because he could not see it.[16]

As soon as Michelangelo arrived in Rome, the dying pope asked to speak with him. The previous year, he had given his favorite artist a new commission for one of the largest single frescos ever painted, this time on the west wall of the Sistine Chapel, behind the main altar. Even as he lay dying, Clement wanted to discuss a few last minute details about the fresco. This fresco was constantly on his mind, for it would be a fresco about the Last Judgment, about the end of all things, about the sudden catastrophe of Christ's return, when the wicked would be separated from the good with a curse. The Last Judgment is described in the Gospel of Matthew, when the Son of Man returns on the clouds of heaven and all will be judged and when, as Jesus said, the last would be first, and the first last, and salvation would depend on the quality of your love. Those with love would be blessed; those without it would be cursed.

> The Son of Man would say: "Depart from me, you evildoers, for when I was hungry, you did not feed me, when I was thirsty, you did not give me drink. When I was sick or in prison, you did not visit me."
>
> And they would ask, "Lord, when did we see you hungry or thirsty or sick or in prison?"
>
> And the Son of Man would say, "As long as you failed to do these things for the least of my brothers and sisters, you failed to do it for me."
>
> And they would be carried off by demons to the eternal fire prepared for Satan and his angels. (Matthew 25:31–46)

This is the world in which Michelangelo embarked on the pope's great commission. The upheaval of the Renaissance gave way to further upheaval as the Reformation began. It was an electric time, abundant with new ideas and new theories, but also accompanied by an increasing sense of fear. It was a climate of political and religious warfare, when politics and church reform collided. Michelangelo stood at the cusp of that change, and his great fresco, the *Last Judgment,* would be a testament to these times.

CHAPTER ONE

The Great Commission

The story of the *Last Judgment* began many years before that last meeting between Pope Clement VII and his favorite artist from Florence, and like so many Renaissance stories, it begins in a garden. Michelangelo's first teacher, Domenico Ghirlandaio, an accomplished fresco painter, began to teach the thirteen-year-old boy the art of *buon' fresco,* though Michelangelo's real talent as a sculptor soon emerged. Realizing this, one of Ghirlandaio's students, Francesco Granacci, took him to see the Medici sculpture garden at San Marco, which Lorenzo had commissioned in order to adorn the Medici library. While there, Michelangelo so greatly admired a sculpture—the *Head of a Faun,* which depicted an ancient faun, its mouth open wide with laughter, and its tongue hanging over its teeth—that he decided to copy it. He begged a bit of marble and some tools from the workmen, and set about carving the stone. However, instead of merely copying the original statue, Michelangelo changed its shape to suit himself, drawing the tongue back into the mouth, and exposing the teeth.

Lorenzo de Medici loved to walk in the garden every morning and evening in order to check on the progress of the work he had commissioned. One morning he came across the bent-nosed teenaged boy polishing a bust of an ancient faun. Lorenzo admired the work and was amazed at the boy's talent. He joked that Michelangelo must have known nothing of old men, because he had carved the figure with a full set of teeth, when anyone knows that by the time men reach old age many of their teeth are gone. Michelangelo waited impatiently for Lorenzo to leave, and when he was alone, he took a hammer and knocked a front tooth out of the sculpture, and then drilled a hole into the gum. Later that evening, Lorenzo walked through the garden again and discovered what Michelangelo had done. He laughed at the boy's cleverness, and in the following days arranged with both Ghirlandaio and Michelangelo's father, Ludovico Buonarroti, to allow the boy to live in the Medici palace with his own children and be raised along with his sons.[1]

During the next forty years, Michelangelo established himself as one of the greatest artists in Europe. He carved the titanic statue of *David* in Florence, painted the ceiling of the Sistine Chapel, lived in Florence, Rome, Bologna, and Venice, all the while absorbing new techniques and new artistic ideas. Before and after the siege of Florence in 1528 and the fall of the short lived republic in 1530, Pope Clement had commissioned him to work on the New Sacristy, which sat opposite the Old Sacristy, of the Church of San Lorenzo in Florence, as well as the Medici chapel and library.

The Medici chapel was a family tomb, and Michelangelo carved two of his most famous sculptures for that project—a statue of a nude reclining man entitled *Day* and of a nude reclining woman entitled *Night.* Both were melancholy figures, which fit Michelangelo's mood after the violent death of the republic, but it was the sculpture *Night* that seemed most mournful, reminding all who saw it of the quick approach of death and the long silence of the tomb.

Clement micromanaged all of these projects from the Vatican, shooting off a letter nearly every day. He directed Michelangelo about which type of wood (walnut) was to be used for the library ceiling and which colors to choose for the walls. He wanted the ceiling of the library vaulted rather than with wooden beams "lest some drunkard, not uncommon with priests, sets fire to the room, spreading to the library."[2] However, he doubted that Michelangelo's plan to put skylights in the library ceiling would work because it would require the hiring of at least two friars to regularly wipe off the dust.[3] His enthusiasm for Michelangelo's art often overflowed its boundaries. At times, Clement would be possessed by a new idea and demand that Michelangelo drop everything and attend to it.

Overcome by work, the artist had grown increasingly despondent and he began to think more about death—his favorite brother, Buonarroto, had died of plague during the siege of Florence, and his father died three years later, leaving Michelangelo to manage the ill-tempered Buonarroti clan on his own. Eventually Clement had to order Michelangelo to take a break and rest. Clement communicated most of the time through Sebastiano Luciani, also called Sebastiano del Piombo.

Sebastiano came from Venice and was a member of the Venetian school of art. He started his professional life as a musician, playing the lute before gatherings of the Venetian upper class, Although musicians were important in Italian society, the real glory was in the fine arts—painting, fresco, and sculpture. After making his name as a

lutenist, Sebastiano turned to painting, and by 1511 he was working
in Rome alongside Raphael on several mythological frescos. Raphael
was a smooth character, handsome and beloved of women, who gathered around him as if he were a rock star. Michelangelo despised him
as Bramante's protégé, and so encounters between Michelangelo and
Raphael were not always cordial.

Sebastiano was part of the pilgrimage of painters who travelled
there to study Michelangelo's wonderful Sistine ceiling, and ended up
working with Raphael instead. When Sebastiano famously quarreled
with Raphael, Michelangelo befriended him, and offered him designs
that Sebastiano turned into finished paintings, particularly the *Raising
of Lazarus*. Sebastiano realized that while he was a competent painter,
he lacked that divine spark that set fire to Michelangelo's work, and
that while his paintings would be celebrated in their own way, they
could not contain the world of human emotions that his friend's did
so naturally.

When Giulio de Medici became Pope Clement VII, he awarded
Sebastiano the office of *piombatore,* the keeper of the seal of state.
It was his job to secure apostolic briefs with the papal seal to ensure
their legitimacy, and he acquired the title "del Piombo" from this
office. In order to get the job, however, Sebastiano had to assume
the habit of a friar, though not the habits of a friar. The job grossed
approximately 800 scudi a year, and Clement split the income
between the two men on the short list. Even though Sebastiano
got the job, he was commanded to hand over 300 scudi a year to
Giovanni da Udine.

While Michelangelo was in Florence, Sebastiano became the
message bearer between Pope Clement and the artist, passing on
Michelangelo's questions and complaints, and acting as interlocutor on
the commission of the *Last Judgment*. In spite of this, Michelangelo's
relationship with Sebastiano was never close; while he remained in
Florence, Friar Sebastiano could befriend him in letters and act as his
agent in the papal court, but the foundation of his friendship with
Michelangelo was developing cracks. Cellini, the gossip of Rome, said

that Sebastiano would disparage Michelangelo in front of others in their circle, a fact that eventually got back to the sensitive Michelangelo.[4]

Like his uncle Lorenzo, Clement was more than tolerant with the touchy Michelangelo. He used to say that when Buonarroti came to visit, he always asked the artist to sit down because he would anyway, with or without permission. No one had ever treated Clement with as much cheek, which oddly enough seemed to please the pope. He read and reread letters Michelangelo sent to him, and whenever his artist sent a letter to someone else at the papal court, Clement insisted on reading it himself, sometimes pocketing the letter as if it were his own.

In 1518, during the reign of Pope Leo X, Michelangelo wrote to the future Clement, then Cardinal Giulio de Medici, outlining his adventures in purchasing marble for statues, and said: "They made me pay sixty ducats more for it than it's worth, pretending they regret it, but saying they cannot contravene the terms of the Bull of sale they had from the Pope. Now if the Pope is issuing Bulls granting license to rob, I beg Your Most Reverend Lordship to get one issued to me too."[5] This was the artist's manner of speaking and writing to Clement even after he became pope. Clement, who was demanding, and even abusive at times with his servants, tolerated so much from Michelangelo and so little from everyone else.

In 1525, two years before the sack of Rome, Clement had the idea that he wanted Michelangelo to make a colossus in Florence, bigger than the *David*. At the time, the sculptor was busy working on another Medici commission but Clement insisted on this colossus to enhance his family's honor. It was partly Michelangelo's fault, for he had foolishly raised the notion of creating large statues by assembling and sculpting blocks of marble rather than sculpting one whole piece. Because these huge statues were hollow inside, unlike single piece sculptures, they could be constructed using architectural techniques, and could be built as large as any building. Clement wrote to Michelangelo through a mutual friend, Giovan Francesco Fattucci, a chaplain at Santa Maria del Fiore in Florence, that he wanted his artist to begin work on a colossus at least 40 braccia (one braccio is equal to a forearm's length, about 28 inches) high, that would be made out of blocks. The pope was completely serious, and Fattucci took care to inform Michelangelo about this new commission. Instead of taking the idea to heart, however, the sculptor fired off a letter to Fattucci that treated the whole idea as a joke:

> I thought that the figure might be sitting, which is hollow underneath, which can conveniently be done with blocks, its rear end coming at such a height that the barber's shop could go underneath, and the rent would not be lost...Then I had another idea, a better idea, even though the figure would have to be much larger, which is still possible because it would be made of blocks. The head could be made hollow, so that it could serve as a campanile for San Lorenzo, much needed. With the bells clanging inside and the sound coming from its mouth, the colossus could be made to appear as if it were crying aloud for mercy.[6]

The Pope didn't find it funny. Through his secretary Pietro Paolo Marzi, he insisted that Michelangelo drop everything and start the colossus. Michelangelo ignored the pope's demands, and the pope gradually became irritated over Michelangelo's continued refusal. For his part, the artist was growing impatient and exhausted due to Clement's ever-growing demands. Even when Marzi sent him a letter reminding him that the pope was serious about his colossus and did not appreciate Michelangelo's humor he ignored it.

Realizing that his demands were accomplishing nothing, Clement sent Michelangelo another letter through Marzi about the importance of existing commissions on the New Sacristy and Library, adding a long postscript in his own hand, using the familiar form of address as they had done as boys. Still irritated, he reminded Michelangelo that popes do not live forever, but he also promised him that he, the pope, would remain patient. Clement ended by promising Michelangelo his friendship and loyalty. Such a personal note coming from an irritated pope to an artisan with such a promise was almost unheard of. Anyone else would have been summarily dismissed for not responding promptly to the pope, but not Michelangelo. After that letter, Clement dropped the entire project and never mentioned it again.

By 1533, Michelangelo wanted to get out of Florence and to begin work in Rome. He had gradually lost enthusiasm for the Medici library and chapel project. His mournful statues of *Day* and *Night* were roughed out and nearing the final stages, but he left them and the tomb statues of the Medici forebears, the *magnifici,* Lorenzo and Giuliano, for others to finish. Clement had run out of money for the project anyway, so the events coincided nicely. Michelangelo was also increasingly concerned about the attitude of Duke Alessandro, the pope's illegitimate son and heir. Alessandro had a tyrannical personality, a vicious temper, and forgave nothing. Despite Pope Clement's pardon for Michelangelo's loyalty to the Florentine Republic following the sack of Rome and temporary ouster of the Medici, Alessandro was openly hostile to the artist because of his participation in the rebellion. If Clement, whose health had been deteriorating since the sack of Rome, died while Michelangelo was in Florence, the duke would have had no qualms about assassinating him. It would be far safer for Michelangelo to be in Rome when Clement passed away. In addition, on one of his trips to Rome the previous year, Michelangelo had met and fallen deeply in love with a young nobleman named Tommaso de Cavalieri.

Michelangelo met Cavalieri in the late autumn of 1532 on his first trip to Rome since he had reconciled with Clement following the rebellion and the siege of Florence and he had returned to Florence. Clement had allowed him to travel to Rome four months of the year to work on the tomb of Julius II, but demanded that he return to Florence and the library for the rest of the year. Sometime in those four months, Michelangelo met Cavalieri and was taken with the young man, who was then around twenty-three years old and a great admirer of the older artist. Michelangelo fell deeply in love with handsome Tommaso, whose face was perfection and whose manners were always flawless. Here was the perfect man, intelligent, artistically talented, well-educated, and the talk of Roman society.

Cavalieri was a Roman nobleman, half Michelangelo's age, and was at first uncertain about the amorous advances of the great man who, for all his fame, still rode around the city on a mule and at the end of the day, slept in his boots. Cavalieri was more conventional than Michelangelo, and wanted a home and family—he married in 1548. However, he soon overcame his fears and reached out to Michelangelo by letter.[7]

In spite of the danger of this romance—what people whispered in the corners could end up as charges of heresy or worse, sodomy—Michelangelo did not try to hide his affection for the young man, writing him letters and passionate poems that he intended for publication.

When Michelangelo returned to Florence to work on the library following the pope's orders, he started a long correspondence with Tommaso, expressing a fire that grew hotter with time and distance, and with the discovery that Tommaso shared his affection. In a letter, Michelangelo wrote to his beloved: "I could not forget your name any more than I can forget the food on which I live, because it nourishes only my body, while your name nourishes both my body and my soul."[8] Michelangelo wrote several drafts of this letter and, typical of the time, cast his passion for Tommaso into terms of religious sentiment. If questioned, he would have said that he was first in love with Cavalieri's soul, and only then in love with his beauty. While in Florence, Tommaso became Michelangelo's source of health, love, and, he believed, his everlasting salvation. In August, the young man wrote back to Michelangelo: "I am certain you can not forget me. Please return as soon as you can and release me from prison, for I keep away from bad companions and want only you."[9]

Over the next few months, they exchanged letters through the mediation of Bartolomeo Angiolini, a Florentine businessman living in exile, and the central figure of a group of exiles opposed to Duke

Alessandro de Medici. While Michelangelo was still living in Florence, Angiolini became his business manager in Rome, and arranged to have the letters carried from Rome to Florence and back again. In this time, partly because of their rising passion, both Michelangelo and Cavalieri, who was an artist in his own right and a talented musician, experienced a flurry of creativity. Michelangelo wrote some of his most passionate poetry, mostly directed to Tommaso with an unabashed fervor bordering on the mystical.

> If the heart can be seen in the face through the eyes,
> I have no other, more apparent sign
> Of my flame, so let these be enough
> My dear lord, to petition for your mercy.[10]

But in the back of Michelangelo's mind was always the awareness of sin. The voice of Savonarola, who Michelangelo remembered as the true prophet, nibbled at his conscience, and in his poetry, his passion flowed first to Cavalieri and then to God.

> O flesh, O blood, O wood, O ultimate pain
> through you may be justified all of my sin,
> in which I was born, just as my father was.
> You alone are good; may your infinite mercy
> relieve my predestined state of wickedness
> so near to death and so far from God.[11]

Oddly, however, Michelangelo did not seem to be concerned about the public censure. Far from warning him, however, his friends, Angiolini and Sebastiano del Piombo, "encouraged and reassured him of Tomasso's love."[12] In a series of chatty letters, Angiolini passed on tidbits of gossip about events in Rome—how Pope Clement, twisted with indecision over the request for an annulment of the marriage of England's King Henry VIII to Catherine of Aragon, cried out in pain; how Clement had decided to journey to Marseilles to assure the marriage of his niece, Catherine; and of Angiolini's own desire to become a poet like Michelangelo, as long as he could do so while cooking sausage and liver. On August 15, he reassured Michelangelo once again that Tommaso "had no other desire in the world than for you to return, for he says that when he is with you he knows he is happy, for having all he desires in this world."[13]

In October 1533, Michelangelo's love for Tommaso produced a series of new sonnets in which he sought to identify himself with the young man and to elevate that passion to new religious heights. This probably had much to do with his already complex self-image that grew even more complex as his love for Cavalieri clashed with his innate religious zeal. He was a true believer at heart, and his poetry revealed the agonies of his soul. This sentiment was so strong that as he painted the *Last Judgment,* he feared that he would be among the damned at Christ's left hand, slouching their way to perdition.

To counteract this feeling, in his poetry he sought to find a place for his earthly love in the heavenly universe. In one of these poems, he condemned the common course of humanity, the rabble who could never understand his feelings and who projected their own prejudices on others, because they could not understand the glory of the human soul and the majesty of God that were reflected in the depths of his love, which would remain undiminished and his desire unblemished.[14]

Apparently, the whispering campaign against him about his relationship with Cavalieri had already begun. Rome was not Florence, and what would be blithely tolerated in Tuscany would be harshly condemned in Rome. This condemnation would only grow with time as the Renaissance waned. The old dichotomy of flesh and spirit had been passed down from Plato and the Greeks. During the Middle Ages, it had been transformed into two opposing inclinations within the soul. The flesh was forever identified with sin, and all physical luxuries were to some degree a collaboration with the Devil.

In a sonnet written for Cavalieri in the summer of 1533, Michelangelo lamented his ambivalence

> This, lord, has happened to me since I saw you
> A bitter sweetness, a yes-and-no feeling moves me;
> Surely it must have been your eyes.[15]

Years later, however, he remarked that he looked forward to death, when he would be free of the passion that had dogged him his whole life.

In one of his sonnets to Cavalieri, Michelangelo paints himself as an old man, desiring to run like a stag, a lynx, or a leopard if he could; and with his dark soul cast by a smith forging metal by fire, he is given strong wings and becomes like the moon which remains invisible until revealed by the sun. With time, Michelangelo's passion for Tomasso cooled, but the two men remained friends until Michelangelo's death, when Tomasso knelt beside Michelangelo's deathbed praying for his soul. All Michelangelo's works from the *Last Judgment* to the end of his life were prayers, and his own deeply felt concern for his many sins lent passion to his depiction of the end of days and the coming perdition.

CHAPTER TWO

Clement's Brainstorm

*I*n June 1533, an unusual lecture took place in the Vatican Gardens, concerning a new model of the heavens. New ideas passed around Europe fairly quickly, even before the easy availability of books. Stories and new concepts spread among the elite, who offered public lectures and disputations, or philosophical debates, while among themselves, they distributed longwinded letters defending or attacking the latest ideas. It is likely that it was through this informal network that Clement first heard rumors about Copernicus. Though his book on the order of the universe *De revolutionibus orbium coelestium* would not be published for another ten years, most of the inner circle of the papal court had already heard his name and had some knowledge of his ideas.

In the late summer of 1496, Copernicus had left Poland and journeyed to Italy, where he entered the University of Bologna to study canon law. He lived in Rome for ten months in 1500 and lectured on astronomy and mathematics.[1] It's not surprising, therefore, that Pope Clement had heard a good deal about Copernicus by 1533. Open-minded to a fault, the pope loved new ideas. With Copernicus, a new vision of nature was about to refashion the medieval universe into the modern. The lecture in the Vatican garden occurred over a series of days, as Johann Albert Widmanstadt, a philosophical and theological consultant for the pope, explained the new Copernican system of the heavens. We know that the lecture occurred because of an unusual inscription on the front page of the *Codex Graecus Monacensis,* a fifteenth-century Greek manuscript about religious life once owned by Widmanstadt. The inscription reads:

> Our Supreme Pontiff Clement VII gave this codex to me as a gift in A.D.1533, in Rome, on the day when, in the presence of Fra Ursino, Cardinal Johannes Salviati, Cardinal Johannes Petrus, Bishop of Viterbo, and Matthias Curtius medical physician, in the garden of the Vatican I explained to him, Copernicus's teaching regarding the motion of the earth.[2]

Since he was still living in Florence, Michelangelo was not in attendance at this meeting, but he was quite friendly with both the pope and with Cardinal Salviati, the son of Jacopo Salviati, the brother-in-law of Lorenzo the Magnificent, and so he had probably heard much about it.

In July 1533, one month after the lecture, Pope Clement had an idea for a new fresco for the Sistine Chapel. He became very excited and spoke about it at length with Sebastiano del Piombo. Clement then commanded Sebastiano to write Michelangelo in Florence and tell him that the pope intended to bestow a wondrous new commission upon him, one that would take place in Rome, thus freeing him from the Medici

Chapel and Library projects, and allowing him to escape the threat of Duke Alessandro. In his letter, Sebastiano had picked up Clement's excitement and wrote to Michelangelo that the pope would "make a contract with you for something such as you never dreamed of…these words were not just talk between us. His Holiness has charged me to report them to you, on his behalf, and note well, they are words of great importance."[3] Sebastiano then said that Clement wanted to meet with Michelangelo to explain this great commission face to face, but did not mention that the pope first wanted to travel to Marseilles to preside at the wedding of his niece Catherine de Medici.

Clement's plan was to leave Rome for France sometime in August, though the trip was later delayed several times. On August 2 Sebastiano sent Michelangelo another letter telling him that it was his great joy to report that the pope wished to stay two or three days in Florence in order to discuss future commissions with him. At the beginning of August, Clement's Florentine secretary, Gian Francesco Bini, wrote to Michelangelo that it was the pope's wish that the artist stay in Florence for the time being in order to finish his work, but that later Michelangelo should choose someone from Rome to complete what he had not done. Michelangelo soldiered on with his work and waited for word from the Vatican, while weeks and then months passed. Through August and on into September the pope delayed leaving, citing bad weather. Finally, he announced his plan to set out soon after September 6, 1533.

Clement had many troubles. Since the sack of Rome, the Holy Roman Emperor had him by the throat. The French and the Spanish refused to deal with each other, refused to make peace, refused to limit their avarice for empire. Clement had to avoid offending the two kings, to the point that he dared not validate the divorce of the English King Henry VIII because Catherine of Aragon was a Hapsburg. Henry was not likely to go to war with the Hapsburgs to protect the pope, so the only thing for Clement to do was deny the divorce and let England leave the Roman Catholic fold. Instead, Clement did what he always did—he dithered. Ostensibly, he was on his way to France to preside at the wedding of his niece to the young Duke of Orleans, who would become Henri IV, the Huguenot prince who chose to become a Catholic to win the crown. However, his other reason for the journey was to try to convince the king of France, Francis I, to make peace. He failed in this, though he still managed to connect his family with both royal families. His niece would marry Henri and Alessandro, the new Duke of Tuscany, would marry the emperor's niece to establish a political balance. After he finally set off, Clement traveled with his company to Pisa by the Sienese route and was delayed there until early October because of bad weather.

Fearing assassination from Florentine Republicans or from family members of those he had tortured and executed during the siege, Clement thought better of traveling to Florence or even through Florentine territory, and sailed instead to France from Livorno to Villafranca. Accompanying him were ships of the Knights of St. John, an escort of French ships, and on his papal barge, nine cardinals, including his nephew Ippolito de Medici and Cardinal Farnese, who would later become the next pope, Paul III.

On his way to France, Clement met with Michelangelo on September 22, 1533, in the town of San Miniato al Tedesco, or San Miniato of the Germans, built on the crown of a hill overlooking the valley of the lower Arno, a short way from Pisa. The road into the town winds up the crest of a hill, rising forward past the wall, past the shops and houses roofed with terra cotta tiles, to the cathedral and bishop's residence at the top, where the conversation took place in the bishop's garden.

The two men walked among the flowers like old friends reunited, discussing grand new ideas. It was likely that at this meeting Clement told Michelangelo all about Copernicus and his new vision of the heavens, and that he wanted to memorialize that idea in art. It is certain that they discussed the fresco at great length, and likely Michelangelo proposed a number of ways that the idea of heliocentrism could be encoded in the work. At first, Clement wanted a resurrection scene, but no one is certain if this meant the resurrection of Christ or the general resurrection of the dead, the last judgment. Because of the terrible events of 1527, it was probably the latter. They also planned a counterbalancing fresco of the fall of the rebel angels over the doorway, but this never happened.

Sailing into Villafranca, he met with Catherine de Medici and then sailed on to Marseilles, arriving on October 12. As a head of state, he entered the city and waited there for the king to arrive on October 13. Then, on October 28, Clement officiated at the wedding. During the lavish celebration that followed, people whispered about the pope's cousin Cardinal Ippolito, who was dressed so splendidly that he outshone the king. Meanwhile, Clement and King Francis met secretly to negotiate their future relations. They agreed to postpone the General Council of the Church. No pope ever wanted to convene a General Council because once all the bishops were assembled, no one could predict what they would do. Because Clement had been born illegitimately, he feared that the council would bring this up and demand that he step down from the papacy. They also decided to put off the excommunication of England's Henry VIII. Some said that Clement also agreed to allow France to ally itself with the Turks in order to defeat the emperor, but this seems unlikely because he feared the Turks almost as much as he did the emperor.

After Clement's return from Marseilles, his interest in the new fresco grew, even as his health declined. Almost immediately after his arrival in Rome, he ordered the ring and vestments to be used for his burial, and quietly announced to the court that he would die soon.[4] This was all the more reason to recall Michelangelo to Rome to begin the great commission. The new fresco would definitely be a Last Judgment, a painting that would capture the terror that the Roman people felt during the sack of Rome.

The *Last Judgment* was as much a theological statement as it was a cosmological one, but the difference between the two disciplines of religion and science was thin during the Renaissance. Cosmology begat theology, and vice versa. A cosmology had to adapt both to the

Christian story and also to the philosophical sentiments of the day. Traditional Last Judgment scenes reflected the Aristotelian love of hierarchies and with the medieval idea of the Great Chain of Being. Everything in the Middle Ages existed in a hierarchy which defined it, shaped it, set it into the scheme of things. Just as there was a greatest flower—the rose, so there was a greatest gem—the diamond. There was a greatest animal—the human being; and the greatest created spirits—the cherubim and seraphim who forever contemplated the mystery of God. At the top God fixed the world in its static order.

This is at the opposite emotional pole to Michelangelo's version, which was more modern in its sensibility. The cosmos here is dynamic, changing, and the end of the world was less a reaffirmation of an eternal order than it was a catastrophe, a swirling, searing, violently charged moment at the end of time in which even the blessed seem agitated and the angels seem to be at war. Everything swirled around the central figure of Christ as the sun, the perfect Neoplatonic God; the blessed and the damned whirled around him like asteroids in orbit around a star. Michelangelo retained a sense of the old hierarchies, but as he did so he transformed them into something new, something brawlingly alive.

Some of these ideas arose from the Neoplatonists, most notably Marsilio Ficino, Lorenzo de Medici's chief philosopher, a humanist who founded the Florentine Academy. Several grand concepts at the heart of Ficino's thought appealed to the Renaissance mind, for both aesthetic and ideological reasons. One concept was that beauty was the way to God, something that was at the center of Michelangelo's spirituality. The soul, consumed by divine brilliance, is seized unknowingly by that brilliance and is drawn upward as if by a hook. The body is a reflection of the soul, and a beautiful body, whether that of a man or a woman, is a reflection of the beauty to be found in the soul.[5] This is why Michelangelo could walk such a fine line between religion and sensuality in his poetry. No one asked if an ugly body meant an ugly soul, but this was implied.

This notion of beauty fed Michelangelo's art and his life as he consciously transformed his erotic feelings to an admiration for the beloved's soul. To attain true happiness, people believed at the time, one must make the ascent through the intellect, rooted in knowledge and love of the elements, and then fly to the immaterial heavens, to the soul without dimensions, to the world of angels who are not born and do not die, and to God—the mystery beyond mysteries.

As Clement's health sank further, his family—Lucrezia Medici Salviati, who ran the papal household, her daughter Maria Salviati Medici, and Cardinal Giovanni Salviati—and his household—his chamberlain, notary, and secretaries—all gathered by his bed. Michelangelo was likely among them. The death of a pope is rarely a private affair.

Clement died on September 15, 1534. Later generations judged him harshly. Clement had risen to power through his wits and his understanding of church politics, but once he sat on the throne of Peter, he seemed unable to chart a straight course and led the Roman Catholic Church from one disaster to another. His indecision had earned him the nickname "*Clemens Pontifex Minimus*"—which everyone in Rome snickered at while he was still alive, and which was scrawled across his tombstone after his death, replacing *Clemens Pontifex Maximus.* People blamed him for the sack of Rome, with some justification.[6] Their pope, their *papa,* their spiritual father had done little to help them as the drunken hordes broke through the city walls and howled through the streets, savaging everything they could find.

His will bequeathed Florence to his illegitimate son Alessandro and everything else to his nephew Ippolito. When his body lay in state, a mob of Romans broke in, intending to drag his body through the streets, and were turned back by the Swiss guards. Cardinal Salviati used all his power to keep the dead pope's tomb undefiled. For weeks, people threw feces at the memorial stone, so that it had to be cleaned every morning. For all the years that generation of Romans lived, they never forgave Clement his sins.

After Clement died, Henry VIII broke with Rome and took the English church with him. Certainly Henry's reasons were dynastic and not theological, but if Clement had taken a more active role in reforming the church, things might have turned out differently. But maybe not. Out of fear, Clement had refused to call a General Council of the Church, which would eventually take place in Trent, in northern Italy, to address Europe's troubles, and that, more than anything, made him a pope of missed chances.

Michelangelo survived Clement by many years, living in Rome through four more papacies, never once returning to Florence. By September 1534, of all his brothers, only Giovansimone and Gismondo remained in that city—and they were his least favorite. His nephew Lionardo and his niece Francesca, the children of his brother Buonarroto, survived in the care of Giovansimone. Michelangelo's nephew Simoni had died around the same time as Michelangelo's father, in 1530, and his old servant Antonio Mini had died in France. There was little left for him in Florence.

CHAPTER THREE

Pope Julius's Tomb

After Pope Clement died, Michelangelo believed that the Last Judgment commission had died as well. He was glad of it because he was determined to return to work on the tomb of Pope Julius II. He had long desired to complete that project, but one pope after another had brushed his project aside for his own reasons. Every pope wanted his piece of the great artist for his own pet projects and each time, to make room for his own desires, the pope would force Michelangelo to accept a new contract for the tomb, shrinking the project's scope bit by bit.

The entire tomb project, later deemed a "tragedy,"[1] was a study in cost overruns and bureaucratic meddling that dated back to 1505. In 1503, Pope Alexander VI Borgia died and the new pope took the name Julius II. The new pope, a della Rovere, was a fierce old man who burned to recapture the lands taken from the papal states by the imperialist Venetians, and to punish those disloyal lords who had made accommodations with the pope's enemies. He gathered his armies for battle, often leading them himself. Everyone around the papal court feared his volcanic temper. When his anger burned, not even bishops were safe from being beaten from the room.[2]

In 1505, two years after his election, Julius summoned Michelangelo from Florence, sending along 100 ducats for his traveling expenses. Michelangelo was coming into artistic maturity, and his reputation as a bold new sculptor had spread all over Europe. Once Michelangelo arrived in Rome, the pope had him hang around idly in the city for months while he decided what he wanted him to do. Finally, Julius commissioned him to design and build the papal tomb. Julius was an old man, and while he possessed a granite constitution, his age reminded him that his death was not all that far away. If he were going to be buried in style, he would have to make preparations. A few months later, Michelangelo presented him with his design. Julius loved the design and ordered his secretary Alemanno Salviati to pay Michelangelo 1,000 ducats to purchase marble for the tomb.

According to Michelangelo's design, the tomb was supposed to be freestanding, and was to be so stupendous that Julius considered redesigning St. Peter's cathedral in order to contain it. He wanted to construct the most lavish tomb in Rome, measuring 34 ½ feet long by 23 feet wide, rising like a church within the church to almost 23 feet in height, with forty statues carved by Michelangelo himself. There would be two angels arching at the entrance, forming a doorway into a temple.

Julius gave Michelangelo five years to complete the project—an optimistic estimate. But Michelangelo, still a young man with a boundless capacity for work, was certain he could finish in that time. With his new commission in hand, Michelangelo set up shop in a house in the area just behind the Castel Sant'Angelo, close to the river.[3] For the next eight months, beginning April 1505 with two helpers and only one horse between them, and a little bit of food, Michelangelo wandered around the quarries of Carrara looking for those perfect blocks of marble that contained just the right forms yearning for Michelangelo to free them with his chisel.

One day, as he was sitting and staring at the mountains surrounding the quarries, a sudden fancy took hold of him. He wanted to carve a giant colossus out of the mountains, something that could be seen by ships at sea, something that would stand as long as the mountains themselves stood.[4] Everyone knew of the great Colossus of Rhodes, one of the wonders of the ancient world, and there was no reason why Italy couldn't have its own colossus. He could see that the shape of the rocks surrounding him would allow him to carve the giant figure with ease, and with a typical Renaissance mindset, he yearned to emulate the ancients, who saw a bit of divinity in a place and had to memorialize it in stone. At twenty-nine, Michelangelo still suffered from a young man's delusions of immortality. Years later, he told Ascanio Condivi, one of his biographers, that he long regretted not following through on that particular dream. Condivi wrote his biography when Michelangelo was an old man. He wrote an official, authorized biography at Michelangelo's request, so as to correct the mistakes that the artist saw in Vasari's account of his life in *Lives of the Artists*.

Michelangelo had quarried and selected enough stone to complete his original design for Julius's tomb, which—though not as big as the Colossus—would be a monumental affair so that even in death Julius would stand prominently among his predecessors. Then he prepared his return to Rome.

Michelangelo sent the marbles on ahead of him, floating them to Rome on a boat. Despite bad weather and several catastrophes and near catastrophes, at the beginning of 1506 Michelangelo finally deposited the great blocks at Ripa. There, they were immediately engulfed by the rising Tiber so that he could not move them the rest of the way to his studio in the Vatican. When the river retreated crowds of Romans gathered round to marvel at their size and beauty.

Meanwhile, the pope's architect Bramante—who was in the process of designing St. Peter's and was in direct competition with Michelangelo in almost everything—whispered in the pope's ear that it was bad luck for anyone to build their tomb before they had died, and that for Michelangelo to continue this project might spread a cloud over his papacy. Bramante didn't particularly like the brash Michelangelo, partly because he was brash and partly because he was from Florence while Bramante was from Urbino. As a typical Renaissance courtier, he set out to undermine any project that the pope had in mind for the Florentine usurper hoping to have him replaced with his own countryman, Raphael. But there was something more to it, something personal. Michelangelo had the bad habit of pointing out all of Bramante's mistakes, and the papal architect hated him for it. The pope never gave Bramante enough money to do a project right, so he had to cut corners, which was obvious to Michelangelo even if not to the pope. If he could have, Bramante would have sent the upstart packing.

Heeding Bramante's advice, Julius decided to divert the money for the tomb to the building of St. Peter's, and Michelangelo suddenly found himself outside of the pope's favor. On Holy Saturday, the day before Easter, he overheard Julius say that he would not pay another penny for marbles, which surprised him. When he asked Pope Julius for the money he needed to begin work on the tomb, Julius told him to come back the next day, which he did, on Monday, then on Tuesday, Wednesday, and Thursday, until on Friday a stableman drove the sculptor from the papal palace, saying, "I have orders not to admit you."[5]

A bishop who witnessed the altercation said to the stableman, "You must not realize who this man is," but the stableman said, "I do know him, but I am obliged to follow the orders of my superiors, without question." As he left, Michelangelo told the stableman "You may tell the pope that from now on if he wants me he can look for me elsewhere."[6] He then marched back to his quarters near Castel Sant'Angelo and ordered that all his tools and furniture be sold. Then, in the middle of the night on April 17, 1506, he rode out of Rome on to Florence.

Full of wrath toward Bramante and his followers, Michelangelo accused them of scuttling his work in Rome, and said that he had feared assassination at their hands. When the pope demanded Michelangelo's return to Rome, he accepted the invitation of Sultan Bayezid II of Turkey to design and build a bridge across the Bosporus on the Black Sea. Julius, on the other hand, did not like the fact that his artist was as *terribile* as he was, and would not be denied Michelangelo's services. Two months after Michelangelo fled Rome, Julius sent a papal brief to the *Signoria* in Florence:

> Michelangelo the sculptor, who left us without reason, and in mere caprice, is afraid, we are informed, of returning, though we for our part are not angry with him, knowing the humors of such men of genius. In order then that we may lay aside all anxiety, we rely on your loyalty to convince him in our name, that if he returns to us he shall be uninjured and unhurt, retaining our Apostolic favor in the same measure as he formerly enjoyed it.[7]

In May, however, Michelangelo sent word to the pope that he would continue his work on the tomb in Florence, where costs were cheaper. Julius learned of this and on July 8 summoned Michelangelo back to Rome. Michelangelo wouldn't go, because he didn't trust Julius and feared his anger. Julius, who saw himself as the master and Michelangelo the servant, summoned him a second time, and then a third, and at that point Piero Soderini, the *gonfaloniere* for life and leader of the *Signoria,* sent for Michelangelo. "You have tried the pope in a way that the king of France would not have done," Soderini told Michelangelo. "However, he is not to be kept waiting any longer."[8] Then he ordered Michelangelo to return to Rome and apologize to the pope.[9]

Pope Julius had left Rome, however, in order to attend to the wars he was waging to restore the lost territories of the papal states. Some of the territories like Bologna and Ferrara had rebelled against papal rule, and Julius felt that it was God's will that they be returned to the fold, by force if necessary. After his conquest of Bologna, Julius summoned Michelangelo, who rode to Bologna "with a rope around his neck," to beg the Pope's forgiveness.[10]

When Michelangelo arrived in Bologna, he went to attend mass at San Petronio where one of the pope's servants saw him and brought him to Julius. The pope was then having his meal at the Palazzo de Sedici, and when he saw Michelangelo, he said to him, "You should have come to us, and yet you have waited for us to come to you."[11] Michelangelo fell on his knees. One of the attending bishops tried to intercede for him, saying that he disobeyed out of ignorance, because artists were often senseless outside their discipline. Julius then said to the bishop, "You abuse him, while we say nothing. You are the ignorant one," and had the man beaten out of the room.[12]

At that point, his anger spent, Julius forgave Michelangelo, and commissioned him to cast a colossal statue of himself in bronze for the city of Bologna, to honor his conquest there. Michelangelo had no experience working in bronze, and told Julius so, but the pope made him do it anyway. Before Julius left Bologna, Michelangelo had produced a clay model of the statue, but puzzled over what to put in the statue's left hand. He had already set the right hand in a gesture of blessing, but in an ambiguous way that almost seemed like a threat.

When the pope visited his artist to see the model, Michelangelo asked him if he wanted to be depicted holding a book. "A book?" said Julius. "A sword! As for me, I am no scholar."[13] Then he jokingly pointed out the gesture of the right hand, and asked Michelangelo if he was blessing or cursing. Michelangelo told him that the statue "threatens this people, Holy Father, lest they be foolish."[14]

Bologna was hot and plague-ridden, and Michelangelo complained bitterly of his misery in letters he sent to his family. He had engaged the services of one of the best bronze artisans in Bologna, and learned about the art of making bronzes as quickly as he could. Working in bronze was a tricky business. If the metal cools too fast, it can crack, and the only thing the artist can do at that point is to melt the statue down and start again. After one failed attempt, he succeeded on February 16, 1508, and on the February 21 set the statue in a niche built for it on the façade of San Petronio. Michelangelo then returned to Florence, and expected that the pope would have no more use for him.

When Julius summoned him once again to Rome in March 1508, he was surprised, but he returned as commanded. Pope Julius had chosen him to paint the vaulted ceiling of the Sistine Chapel, the pope's official chapel, which sits on the other side of a small courtyard to the right of St. Peter's in Rome. Michelangelo protested that he was no painter, but a sculptor, but the pope insisted. Michelangelo protested again and again so many times that Pope Julius grew angry, and Michelangelo was forced to prepare the ceiling to be painted. For the next four years, he labored to master the difficult art of *buon' fresco* (good fresco) a painting technique he had not used since his days in the workshop of Domenico Ghirlandaio, the Renaissance painter to whom Michelangelo's father had apprenticed him at an early age. In *buon' fresco,* ground pigments are painted into thin wet plaster so that the colors soak in and fuse with the wall and ceiling surfaces; the technique requires rapid brush strokes to create images before the plaster dries. With each new image, his skill in the art increased exponentially. At the beginning, when he painted Noah's flood, the figures were wooden and lifeless, but by the end, with his painting of the prophet Jonah, he had developed a dynamic new presentation of the human form, one that artists would imitate for centuries. Raphael once visited the chapel with Bramante while the work was in progress and was so impressed, he immediately borrowed some of Michelangelo's techniques.

The ceiling images told the story of salvation history, how the lives and deeds of ancient biblical patriarchs and prophets paved the way for the coming of the Messiah. The most famous image is the *Creation of Adam,* in which God is an old man with a muscular body, reaching out from heaven to touch the finger of the languid, equally muscular Adam, just then coming to life. Even though God was represented as the source and cause of all things in the fresco, he was not the central character, for the main theme of the ceiling of the Sistine Chapel was the heroic spiritual history of the human race, from Adam to Jesus.

This was Christian humanism at its best, optimistic about the future, treating the sins and foibles of humanity as wounds in the soul rather than causes for damnation. There were also fools and geniuses, prophets and holy men painted into the mix. He also painted the five Roman sibyls in various parts of the fresco. In the case of the Cumaen Sibyl, he painted an outsized, muscular woman with bad eyesight. One of the two children accompanying her "makes the fig," at her, placing the thumb between the second and third fingers in a fist, the Renaissance version of giving someone the finger. Michelangelo was not above planting an obscene joke in his work, even in the official chapel of the pope.

Several times during the painting of the fresco, Michelangelo's insubordination drove Julius into violent rages, once to the point of taking a stick to his back. The impatient Julius stopped by the Sistine Chapel every day and demanded to know when Michelangelo would finish. Michelangelo shouted back, "When I can!" Enraged, the pope shouted back, "You want me to have you thrown off the scaffolding?"[15] Michelangelo muttered to himself that the pope would not throw him off the scaffolding, put away his paints, ordered the scaffolding removed, and declared the painting finished. Julius was thrilled with Michelangelo's work, as was all of Rome, but the pope could not help making a comment about the lack of gold leaf on the work, worrying that people might find it poor. Michelangelo told him that the people depicted there were poor also.[16]

By 1513, Julius informed his master of ceremonies that his frail health would prevent him from presiding at public ceremonies. It was time to turn his attention to his tomb. After Michelangelo's return to Rome during the first months of 1513, the artist negotiated the use of a house and land on the Macel de Corvi, or Raven's Lane, the house that would be his residence in the city for the rest of his life. It was purchased for him by the della Rovere family, who pressed him to continue working on Julius's tomb after the pope's death.

On May 6 of that year, Michelangelo signed a new contract for the tomb with Cardinal Leonardo Grosso della Rovere, the archbishop of Agen, and the other executors of Julius's estate. In his letters he declared that the new design for the tomb would be larger than the first. There would still be forty figures, but these would be colossal. The great difference was that the new design called for the tomb to be attached to one of the walls of the basilica rather than to be freestanding. In this contract, the price went from 10,000 ducats to 16,500 ducats—and the time Michelangelo had to complete the entire work was seven years rather than five. The contract also stated that Michelangelo would undertake no other commissions that would distract him from the tomb, and that he was to work on that project and that project alone. During the next three years, the new pope, Leo X, left Michelangelo in peace so that he could continue with the tomb. The pope was on good terms with Francesco Maria della Rovere, Julius's nephew, who was the reigning Duke of Urbino. During this period, Michelangelo completed his great statue, *Moses* that he intended for the tomb, as well as the two *Captives,* which are now in the Louvre. Everything was going well when suddenly—the Duke of Urbino refused to join with Leo in a war against France in Lombardy—everything fell apart. In retaliation, the pope excommunicated him, took the Duchy of Urbino away from him, and gave it to his own nephew, Lorenzo de Medici. This effectively canceled the contract that Michelangelo had signed with the della Rovere family and sent the project back into limbo.

On July 8, 1516, the executors of Pope Julius's estate drew up a second contract with Michelangelo, one that drastically reduced the size of the tomb project. This time, the family expected only 20 statues by Michelangelo's own hand, and they gave him nine years to complete the project. It had become clear to everyone that Michelangelo's reputation had grown to such a degree that he was no longer completely in control of his commissions. Everyone, popes as well as kings, desired his service, and it would no longer be possible to monopolize it. Moreover, the executors had come to realize that the project was too grandiose, that such a huge tomb, whether in St. Peter's or elsewhere, would create insurmountable problems. The cost would remain the same, and in one of his letters Michelangelo acknowledged receipt of 3,000 ducats. He was also given the use of the house on the Macel de Corvi, rent-free. In a letter dated June 16, 1515, Michelangelo wrote, "I must make a great effort here this summer to finish the work as soon as possible, because afterwards I anticipate having to enter the service of the Pope."[17] It was becoming apparent that his own special relationship with the Medici family would eventually cause problems for his completion of a tomb that celebrated the della Rovere family.

Michelangelo then received a commission from Pope Leo to design a new façade for the church of San Lorenzo in Florence. Once again, work on the tomb had to be put aside. At the time some people criticized Michelangelo for accepting this commission when he still had the tomb to finish. But Michelangelo resented the new tomb contract being more or less forced on him by the agents of the della Rovere, and in a fit of independence, he signed up once again with the Medici. This would cause him enduring trouble. Whatever bad karma he earned for his disloyalty to the della Rovere, he paid for it three times over in the years to come.

From the end of 1516 to March 1520, Michelangelo was completely entwined with the affairs of Pope Leo, especially after the pope provided him with another new commission: to rebuild the sacristy at San Lorenzo in addition to the façade. He soon realized that he had made a mistake and that he was now far more involved with the Medici than he wanted to be. In 1520, the pope canceled his contract for the façade and set him to work on the new sacristy.

Understandably, Michelangelo had made little progress on Julius's tomb, other than blocking out the various figures from the marble. Then, in December 1521, Leo died only five months before the tomb was to be finished. Michelangelo was left on his own, for the pope who had taken him away from the tomb project could no longer run interference for him with the della Rovere. Suddenly, the della Rovere were once again ascendant. Francesco Maria della Rovere regained his duchy, and the new pope, Adrian VI, was no friend of the Medici. He was an ascetic reformer from Holland, humorless and unappreciative of art. He immediately cancelled all contracts with artists, cancelled all spectacles, and shut down theaters and secular diversions of all sorts. The Romans hated him for it. The second tomb contract expired on May 6, 1522, and the newly empowered heirs of Julius clamored for Michelangelo to finish the work, and if he could not, to repay the money plus interest. Michelangelo, on the other hand, was as interested in completing the tomb as the della Rovere, and he told everyone that as early as 1518 he had been deeply troubled about his neglect of the project.

Michelangelo's friends gathered around him and defended him against his critics. Those who had any influence tried to intervene with the della Rovere. In November 1522, Jacopo Salviati, wrote to him and expressed his deep affection and his desire to lend him his full support. Salviati had met with Girolamo Staccioli da Urbino, who was the protonotary of Cardinal Aginensis, the late executor of Julius's estate. Pope Adrian had his secretary prepare a *motu proprio,* which is a document of the pope's own initiative and signed by him, against Michelangelo, ordering him to complete the tomb any way he could. The *motu proprio* was probably never signed, however, and for the next four years, long after Adrian had died and been replaced by Clement VII, the two sides wrangled, with charges and counter-charges, and endless negotiations over details.

In 1526, the della Rovere prepared a lawsuit against Michelangelo, which so upset him that he wrote to a friend, Giovanni Spina, and said that he wanted to surrender, proclaim his guilt, and offer to repay at least part of the money so the heirs of Julius could hire someone else. His friends, notably Jacopo Salviati, dissuaded him and opened negotiations for a third contract.[18] The della Rovere agent, Girolamo Staccioli, took sick, so the matter was tabled until December 8, 1526. In the end, Michelangelo failed to be released from the 1516 contract that so burdened him.

Soon after this exchange, the sack of Rome and the siege of Florence crushed the delicate negotiations and sent all the parties running for their lives. When things settled in 1531, Sebastiano del Piombo wrote to Michelangelo in Florence saying that he had met a fellow painter named Girolamo Genga who told him that the Duke of Urbino wanted to make peace with him, and that he was willing to send the remaining 8,000 ducats to finish the task on Julius's tomb but feared he would lose both money and tomb and was furious. Genga suggested that the project be reduced once again so that Michelangelo could finish it while working on other projects, and Sebastiano wrote to Michelangelo to suggest this.[19] Soon after he had received the title of *piombatore,* he wrote once again to Michelangelo, saying that the duke did not have the money to pay for the big tomb that had been negotiated with Cardinal Aginensis but he could pay for a reduced tomb and even transport the marbles that had been roughed out in Florence to Rome where the tomb would be built.[20] Michelangelo replied that he would prefer to hand back the money and let someone else finish the tomb because he was heartily sick of the whole business and the shame that went with it.[21] Sebastiano said that the heirs wanted a tomb from his hand and no others and expected such, and that they would never agree to the tomb being handed over to someone else.

Over the years, the monument had shrunk in size until it was only a single wall tomb with six statues by Michelangelo's hand. As Michelangelo's position in Florence grew more dangerous under the vengeful Duke Alessandro, he schemed to find ways to stay in Rome and complained to Clement about his unfinished debt to the della Rovere, which he considered to be a debt of honor. He exaggerated this debt in his letter to Clement but the pope already knew of the bad blood between his son Alessandro and Michelangelo.[22] Ultimately Pope Clement allowed Michelangelo to come to Rome for four months a year to work on the tomb, and a new contract was written.

Florence had lost all joy for Michelangelo since the deaths of his father and favorite brother, Buonarroto, and since the last embers of the Florentine Republic had been extinguished by the restoration of the Medicis and Duke Alessandro. The arrests and executions proceeded apace, and while Michelangelo had the protection of Pope Clement, he knew that he could be the victim of an unfortunate accident, or come down with a sudden "stomach ache" that would kill him.

Alessandro was the consummate spoiled brat given too much power too early. Some said he was mad, but in truth he was acting the role that had been given him: the unpredictable tyrant of a rebellious city, the embodiment of the idea that if you cannot win the people's hearts, then rule by fear. Machiavelli had known this about Florence and about the Medici, for he too had suffered torture at their hands. Like the Este in Ferrara, the Medici had fallen far from the glory days of Lorenzo the Magnificent. Not one member of the ruling family was of legitimate birth, and that included Clement. Few of them possessed any real charisma, as Lorenzo had, and they lacked his understanding of the Florentines. Alessandro rode the people like a mule, whipping and kicking them whenever he could. The fact that he was eventually assassinated by his own cousin says much about his personality.

Alessandro had harbored a great hatred for Michelangelo for years because of his role in the rebellion, and because he had been declared untouchable by the pope. Perhaps there was something deeper behind this animosity. Perhaps, unlike Lorenzo and Clement, Alessandro had little patience with the brusque artist, and thought of him as a workman, and hated him for the lack of respect that he perceived the artist bore him. The resentment was only fueled when Alessandro asked Michelangelo to ride out with him and one of his administrators to look over the progress on the new fort that would dominate the city and Michelangelo begged off, saying that the pope had not commanded him to do so. Then he returned to his work. He had no interest in helping the Medici secure their power over Florence, and he feared that Alessandro was planning an accident for him on the way to the site.[23]

Meanwhile, the della Rovere family were again grousing about the delay on the tomb. Vasari said that not a day went by without some agent of the duke pestering Michelangelo about the tomb. The duke's representative, Girolamo Staccioli, spread the word that Michelangelo had embezzled the duke's money, that he wanted to sell the house on the Macel de Corvi that the della Rovere family had given him to finish the tomb, and then rush through the commission in short order. None of this was true: From his letters, it is clear that nothing weighed heavier on Michelangelo's spirit than the unfinished tomb. Clement had kept him far from Rome, unwilling to bend to his favorite artist's sense of honor, using his participation in the rebellion in Florence against him, fastening him ever more securely to Medici commissions.

The marble that he had purchased were still sitting in the rain at Ripa. Michelangelo worried that they would eventually be ruined and he would have to buy new marble for the tomb, something he couldn't afford. Furthermore, the della Rovere family had launched a whispering campaign against him. The papacy of Julius had been their turn at the table, and a great monument to Julius was a monument to the entire family. The Duke of Urbino, Francesco Maria della Rovere, had let it be known through his agents that Michelangelo had accepted 10,000 scudi to complete the tomb but had failed to do so, and that he owed the family 16,000 scudi[24] for money and facilities already invested.

In 1532, the Duke's ambassador, Gianmaria da Modena, in collusion with a local notary, took advantage of the fact that Michelangelo had been sent to Florence by Pope Clement and rewrote the contract to favor the Duke. When Michelangelo read this revised document, he found that the ambassador had added an extra thousand ducats to Michelangelo's debt and then piled on the use of the house that the duke had given him in Rome.

Night after night, Michelangelo lost sleep, and in a September 1533 letter to Bartolomeo Angelini he claimed that he had "aged twenty years and dropped twenty pounds."[25] As a result, he sank further into depression, until he suddenly announced to his friends that he was going to sell his workshop in Florence, along with its marble, and run away. This was typical of Michelangelo when he was under pressure—his friends reminded him that running away would solve nothing. When the panic subsided, he could see the truth in what they said, and returned sullenly to work on the Medici library.

Michelangelo had traveled to Rome several times in 1532—in April, August, and September—and in November 1533, ostensibly to work on the tomb for the della Rovere. He had watched with some fear as Clement's health waned. He was back in Florence for only four months in 1534, and then left for Rome for a final time in September. Clement's approaching death was reason enough for the move, and Michelangelo would never return to the city that had given him life and art. With the death of Clement, all of Michelangelo's papal commissions were frozen until they could be approved by Clement's successor. With the coming of a new pope, Michelangelo hoped that he could drop the Medici commissions, including the *Last Judgment*, and return to finish the tomb.

When Clement died, Michelangelo felt free for the first time in years. He was free of the Medici and their incessant demands, free to pursue the one project that had been hanging over his head for 30 years. Now Michelangelo hoped his honor would finally be assuaged.

The cardinals meeting in conclave on February 29, 1534 to elect the next pope, closed the doors and commenced politicking. That very night, they elected the man everyone assumed would be elected: Alessandro Farnese, who took the name Pope Paul III. From an ancient Roman family that had come from the region around the lake at Bolsena, he had been the bishop of Ostia and the dean of the College of Cardinals. He was Clement VII's choice as his successor and the oldest candidate to be considered.

The Romans liked Paul III because he was the first Roman citizen to be elected pope since Martin V in the Middle Ages. When they heard about the election, the Roman citizens received it with joy and celebration.[26] The cardinals liked him because he was the consummate insider. He was a man with a Renaissance mind, and his election seemed to cast the glories of the Renaissance in the teeth of reform. As a Roman aristocrat, he was the child of years of local corruption. His sister Giulia, a noteworthy beauty, had once been the mistress of Alexander VI, the Borgia pope who wanted to hand over the church to his sons and daughters. Alessandro owed his rise in church politics to that liaison, which earned him the name "Cardinal Petticoat" in the more frivolous circles of the Vatican bureaucracy.

Farnese knew both the Holy Roman Emperor and the King of France and, surprisingly, had won the admiration of both. Everyone liked him it seemed, but no one thought of him as a reformer, as they had of the dour Pope Adrian VI, the former bishop of Utrecht in the Netherlands, who has been pope for eighteen months in 1522. Nobody in Rome really liked reformers, because they tended to be too straight-laced for their tastes. What they didn't recognize was that Pope Paul III was intelligent enough to understand that the winds of reform were blowing across Europe. Those old Christian values—temperance, mortification, self-abnegation, the conquest of the flesh—were coming back into vogue. Neither pope nor emperor could pretend that these ascetic tendencies didn't exist. The party was over.

Pope Paul III was seven years older than Michelangelo, and, like the artist, had spent some of his youth in the house of Lorenzo the Magnificent. Like Michelangelo, he had witnessed the reform movement of Savonarola and had observed the excesses of the Renaissance popes. As the oldest man in the College of Cardinals, he was also the richest. He had fathered four children by the same mistress when he was a cardinal and by the time he rose to the papal throne had five grandchildren on whom he doted with nepotistic fervor, appointing one of his sons Duke of Parma and two of his grandsons, Alessandro Farnese and Ascanio Sforza, to the College of Cardinals. As a cardinal, he loved fine wine and rich food, once feasting Pope Leo X with a banquet in which one course consisted entirely of peacocks. Soon after becoming pope, he built a magnificent palace in Rome for his family, the Palazzo Farnese, which is still standing.

Pope Paul III was a transitional figure, nevertheless, a man who at once loved the arts and yet wanted to reform the church. One of the first things he did was to signal that he wanted to call a general Council of Bishops, the only institution that could question papal authority, in order to rid the church of its many abuses. Clement had been unwilling to do so because he feared the personal consequences. For years, he had stalled the council, even though the Emperor Charles V wanted it convened in order to combat the Lutherans. There was a general sense that what the Protestants had claimed about the Catholic Church was partially true—Renaissance popes and bishops had lived profligate lives. While the openness of the Renaissance was a great strength—an openness of mind to new ideas in a way that appeals to modern secularists— that same openness had allowed the church to become the playground of ambitious Italian families, who used the papacy to establish family empires and commission monuments to their own greatness.

Early on in his reign, Pope Paul III published a papal bull entitled *Sublimus Dei,* which argued against the enslavement of the native peoples of the New World. He also approved the founding of the Society of Jesus. The Jesuit order, as it became known, was instrumental in promoting the Counter-Reformation, otherwise known as the Catholic Reformation, and sent missionaries into the New World, to Asia, and to the most difficult mission of all, the aristocracy of Europe. Ignatius of Loyola, the society's founder, insisted that his men be well-educated, for like Pope Paul III, he was a man with a Renaissance mind and a reformer's heart.

When Michelangelo was summoned by Paul III, he asked for permission to return to the tomb and to abandon all other commissions that had been placed upon him until the tomb was finished. Michelangelo reckoned that he could argue with the new Pope as he had done with his predecessors. At his audience, he explained that the della Rovere family were justifiably incensed that he had not finished the project after all these years, and that he felt honor bound to complete the work before he died. While he was aging, Michelangelo was still a robust man, able to work for long hours without collapsing. The della Rovere family, he argued, had a prior claim on his service, because they had already signed a contract negotiated with him during the reign of Clement VII.

But Pope Paul had a choleric personality, forceful and sometimes dangerous. With a long beard, which had become the fashion for popes and cardinals after Clement grew one as a sign of mourning for the downfall of papal power, he looked a bit like Michelangelo's old patron, Pope Julius. He acted like him, too. He surprised Michelangelo by suddenly raging at him. He said, "for thirty years now, I have desired the service of Michelangelo, and now that I am Pope, may I not indulge myself?" Michelangelo was clearly taken aback by this outburst. He knew from long experience that angry popes were not to be trifled with. But the pope's outburst wasn't over. "Where is this contract?" he said. "I will tear it up." And he did just that. There was no doubt that Pope Paul had the power to do this, because while a pope was alive, he had the power to do whatever he wanted, but as soon as he died, the Vatican administration including all contracts and agreements were reset to zero, and the new pope had to confirm each one. The della Rovere family, it seemed, would have to wait just a bit longer for the tomb.

Michelangelo considered fleeing Rome for Genoa, then under the protection of the Bishop of Aleria who had been appointed by Pope Julius and had befriended the artist. The bishop offered him sanctuary in a monastery under his control, a place near the quarries of Carrara, his main source of marble, and also fairly close to the sea so that he could transport the marble blocks. Michelangelo's other plan was to sneak out of Rome and go to Urbino, where he would enjoy the protection of the duke, and where he found the peace and serenity of the city to be a balm for his soul. He even purchased a house through one of his agents. But he soon abandoned these plans and remained in Rome, because he feared the power of the pope, whose arm was long and who could snatch him from whatever hiding place he might burrow into. Besides, he reasoned, Pope Paul was an old man and he couldn't last that long. Paul surprised him, however, by living on another fifteen years.

As it turned out, the Farnese pope was a great deal like Pope Julius. Although he was not a soldier, he was an able administrator and understood the sensitivities of artists. On one hand, he refused to let Michelangelo out of his service, but on the other, he appointed him the official artist and architect to the papal court, with a salary of 1,200 scudi a year, a tidy sum. In 1544, Pope Paul replaced both the Florentine florin and the Venetian ducat with the scudo, which had slightly more gold in it, and so Michelangelo's shiny new salary set him into a higher class than he had ever been before. With Michelangelo's appointment as papal artist and architect, he had become a man of means. Half of his income would be drawn from tolls taken from the ferry crossing the Po River, and the other half would come from the papal exchequer.

Pope Paul III also understood that artists need to be watched over, and one day, attended by ten cardinals, he came to call unannounced on Michelangelo in his house. Finding him home, he asked to see the cartoon that Michelangelo had prepared for the fresco that Clement VII had asked him to paint in the Sistine Chapel. A gaggle of cardinals followed after, oohing and aahing over the statuary. The cardinal from Mantua gazed at the statue of Moses and said, "Surely, the statue by itself is enough to honor the tomb of Julius." Pope Paul was deeply impressed with the cartoon that Michelangelo showed him for his design of the *Last Judgment,* and he insisted once again that he return to work on the fresco and set aside the tomb project, or at least set it aside while he worked on the painting.

But Michelangelo could be as stubborn as any pope and he had become tired of the incessant demands of his various patrons. Cautiously, he stood his ground against the desires of Pope Paul and insisted that he be allowed to finish the tomb project before he took on any other commissions. The pope returned Michelangelo's obduracy in kind and said, "Don't worry. I will arrange for the Duke of Urbino to accept three statues from your hand, rather than the six. The other three can be passed on to other sculptors to complete for you." So Michelangelo had to accept one more contract, one that the pope negotiated directly with the agents of the duke on his behalf.

Michelangelo could have considered the affair closed and that he was free of all responsibility for the tomb and the last three statues; however, he insisted on paying for them himself and deposited 1,580 ducats in the Strozze Bank for that purpose. Finally, the tomb was finished, though it was not set up in St. Peter's as Michelangelo had originally proposed but in the church of San Pietro in Vincoli, a favorite church of Pope Julius. It was made in the standard form, as a wall niche decorated by six statues, dominated by Michelangelo's *Moses*. Ascanio Condivi later said that in spite of the fact that Michelangelo's original plan had been so changed, and that the tomb had been botched by one pope after another, it was still the most impressive tomb in Rome. In a city like Rome, with so many tombs of so many great men, that is saying a great deal.

The cardinal of Mantua was correct in saying that the *Moses* alone would do honor to the memory of Pope Julius, for there Moses sits with the tablets of the law in his hands, his face aged with worry, resting his chin on his left hand, as one lost in thought. His face, full of struggle, seems to be on the verge of movement. This was one of the great discoveries of Michelangelo's art. He would catch his figures not in any active movement but in the instant before, *contrapposto*, twisted with tension like a coil. Even those characters that represented contemplation were full of latent activity. On either side of Moses are two female figures, sisters from Dante's *Divine Comedy*. On his right, Rachel represents the Contemplative Life, with her face raised to heaven. On his left, Leah represents the Active Life, holding a mirror to show that all of our actions should be taken with self-knowledge and a garland of flowers, just as Dante depicts her in his *Purgatorio*.

The effect that Clement, and later Paul, wanted to have on the visitors to the pope's own chapel was to cast Renaissance excesses as well as Protestant reformers under the shadow of the triumphant Christ.

Two sketches still exist of these early plans for the fresco. One is in the Musée Bonnat in Bayonne, France, showing a seated Christ with Mary kneeling nearby. The later study is in the Casa Buonarroti in Florence and shows a nearly finished version of the fresco.

As a result of the pope's visit, Michelangelo no longer needed to fret over the tomb that he so much wanted to finish, the Duke of Urbino had to accept one more contract, and Pope Paul III had satisfied Michelangelo's honor so that the pope could indulge himself. Everyone seemed satisfied, or at least content.

CHAPTER FOUR

The Altar Wall

$\mathcal{A}$rtists can be as stubborn as popes. For the few months before the signing of the final contract for the *Last Judgment*, Michelangelo secretly worked on the tomb while pretending to be working on the design for the fresco. He would often doodle half-heartedly on the models and sketches during the day, and then steal off at night to work on the statues for the tomb. Even after he had signed the new contract, Michelangelo carried the burden of his dishonor, and purposely delayed the preparation for the *Last Judgment*.

His heart wasn't in it. Another fresco was the last thing he wanted to do, no matter how many popes and cardinals praised his sketches to heaven. His mind hadn't yet settled into the project.

The final design for the tomb pricked his conscience. No one was happy with it—Michelangelo hated it because it fell so far short of his original concept. His early biographer, Ascanio Condivi, who based his writing mostly on personal interviews with Michelangelo, supplemented by the memories of trustworthy men and believable texts,[1] called the final form of the tomb "patched up and reworked."[2] Because the tomb was not ready when Julius died, the family had entombed him in a niche in St. Peter's beside his uncle Pope Sixtus IV, the builder of the Sistine Chapel. During the sack of Rome in 1527, Julius's bones were desecrated by the imperial soldiers. When Michelangelo finally finished the tomb in 1545, the della Rovere family decided to keep Julius's body in St. Peter's, so that to this day the famous tomb of Pope Julius II remains empty.

Once the tomb was finished, Michelangelo found himself once again fully in the service of a powerful pope. Pope Paul III had ensured Michelangelo's attachment to him by giving him an important title and a substantial salary. Even so, the artist moped around Rome, delaying the preparation of the fresco for months. Perhaps he felt that the project was too much for him at his age; fresco painting is a young man's game and Michelangelo was in his sixties. But this is unlikely, since he was perfectly willing to work on the tomb, which was sculpture, also a young man's game.

In 1535, he had a falling out with his long-time friend and supporter Sebastiano del Piombo, which caused a further delay in the painting that lasted nearly a year. It is charitable to think that both Pope Paul and Sebastiano were concerned about Michelangelo's age, and that Pope Paul allowed himself to be persuaded by Sebastiano to have the wall prepared for oil painting on that account. Unlike *buon' fresco* painting, which must be done in day-long sprints to complete each section by the end of that day before the surface dries, oil painting can be done at the artist's leisure, a bit here and a bit there until the work is complete; if something doesn't work, you paint over it. Still, *buon' fresco* endures in a way that oil paint does not, because the fresco pigment becomes part of the wall, while oil painting lies on the dry (*secco*) surface. Sebastiano couldn't see the problem in painting the wall in oils rather than fresco, but Michelangelo strongly disagreed with this proposed solution.

Michelangelo had numerous faults, faults that he was well aware of and that tormented him. He was grumpy, touchy; he worried incessantly about money, even when he was well off, and he worried about his reputation all the time. Apparently, the more people praised him and his work, the more insecure he became. One of the worst of these faults was his tendency to take offense over slights, both real or imagined, and then break off all contact with the offender. He often interpreted the largesse of popes as impositions, and he saw himself as the unwilling victim of papal ambition. If he felt his honor was at stake, if he felt insulted even over a trifle, he could turn his back on long-term friends.

Sometimes Michelangelo manufactured disagreements for that purpose or blew on some ember of an imagined offense until it caught fire, and then proclaimed to everyone how great the insult had been and how much he had suffered. Whether this was true in the case of his dispute with Sebastiano is uncertain. What is certain is that Vasari reports in his life of Sebastiano that after Sebastiano dared to order the altar wall prepared for oil painting, Michelangelo perceived this as an insult and never forgave him.[3]

Michelangelo's touchiness could have been an inherited trait rather than the result of his artistic temperament. His father, Lodovico, was certainly a difficult man. Artistic temperament and the artistic lifestyle, however, may have exacerbated the trait. One day in 1534, Michelangelo spent the morning in conversation with his friends Luigi del Riccio, Antonio Petroneo, and Donato Giannotti. At noon, they all agreed to return to their homes for the afternoon meal and then to gather again later. Del Riccio, who was wealthy and lived in the nearby Palazzo Strozzi, invited all to his house for the meal. Michelangelo refused, saying that he had to return to his work and could not spend more time in conversation. His three friends objected, asking him why he would want to leave them and return to work when the conversation was going so well. Michelangelo said that he was leaving not because he did not care for his friends, but because he cared too much for them. His desire to leave his friends came from fear of too much attachment; being in their presence for more than one morning would make it difficult for him to return to his isolation, and he needed to return to his own house, to his own studio, where he could pursue his lonely work. For Michelangelo, even the presence of his friends was more like a love affair than a companionship. There was always a note of drama in his relationships, especially with men, to the point that their presence became an exquisite agony, like love. Michelangelo had to leave his friends in order to keep his internal equilibrium.

> Anything beautiful to my eyes
> passes through them instantly into my heart[4]

It wasn't just physical beauty that attracted him; it was also the beauty inside, the spiritual beauty that he found in each soul. This would become especially true later on in his friendship with Vittoria Colonna. Michelangelo lurched back and forth between his loneliness and his desire to the point that when he was with his friends, he desired to be alone, and when he was alone, he desired to be with his friends. This pendulum swing in his desires was especially potent in the company of Tommaso Cavalieri, the man whom Michelangelo loved most in the world. Even he was at the mercy of the artist's moods. A letter from Tommaso Cavalieri to Michelangelo pleaded with him to explain the sudden distance of his demeanor. Michelangelo apparently had taken offense at something that Cavalieri had done or said and had retreated into an aggrieved silence, but Michelangelo in true passive-aggressive fashion refused to tell his friend what it was.

Michelangelo's exquisite love pains seem almost adolescent today, the kind of thing we all felt in high school, the yearning of unrequited love, almost like some country-western song. Still, it was a characteristic of the Renaissance when illicit romance could lead one to tragic illness, even death, at least according to the poets.

By his own admission, Michelangelo had an addictive personality when it came to human relationships. This explains his long silences when he felt aggrieved. In a letter from his friend Francesco da Sangallo, an architect, written in 1524, Sangallo speaks of his recent meetings with Michelangelo when the latter met him with sour looks and angry faces, without explaining the reason for his anger, and without giving Sangallo a chance to explain. The storm passed only after Sangallo insisted on seeing Michelangelo and demanded an explanation for his anger. He assured Michelangelo that he would give up every other friendship rather than lose his, and that he would always see Michelangelo as a father to him. Sangallo got his audience and was able to heal the friendship.[5]

Nevertheless, Michelangelo did not suffer fools and incompetents gladly. While he was working on the *Last Judgment,* he employed only his trusted assistant Amadore Francesco d'Urbino, who had worked with him for years and understood his quirks. He distrusted assistants in general, and nearly all of his workers found it difficult to deal with his perfectionism. The seeming impossibility of working alongside a creative genius drove many of his assistants away. "We are hard put to it with a hundred eyes on them to keep one of them at work."[6]

Michelangelo was able to heal his wounded pride in many cases, except on those occasions when the break came from a difference of artistic vision. Unlike Michelangelo, whose gifts lay in capturing the panoply of human emotion and catching the instant of greatest drama, Sebastiano liked to experiment with new artistic media. Oil painting had been growing in popularity, and Sebastiano practiced it in his portraits of great men. With the pope's permission, he ordered that the altar wall of the Sistine Chapel be prepared for oil paints by lathering on a coating of plaster mixed with resin, a laborious and expensive process.

Michelangelo kept silent about this for several months and didn't seem to care, even when the workman had nearly finished. One hypothesis is that Michelangelo considered painting the fresco in oils just to distinguish it from his already famous ceiling, but he didn't like the way the light reflected off the wall. He was determined to return to what he knew best, *buon' fresco*. More likely, Michelangelo's silence was a stalling tactic, to allow him to delay the fresco painting while he worked on the statues for the tomb. Certainly, given his personality, there was more than a note of vengeance in Michelangelo's silence, a snipe at the pope and at Sebastiano's arrogance in preparing the wall without consulting him.

When Pope Paul, with Sebastiano's urging, finally insisted that the new work be done in oils, Michelangelo insisted right back. He had probably made up his mind to work in fresco some months before and, when pushed, demanded his way. In a fury, Michelangelo told the pope that oils were for women and slugabeds like Sebastiano and that he would work only in fresco. The difficulty of painting in *buon' fresco* was balanced by the longevity of the work. Also, the fact that *buon' fresco* was physically and artistically demanding made it a form for masters while painting in oils could be accomplished by dilettantes as well as by accomplished painters.

The art of wall painting dates back to between 15,000 and 20,000 BCE as evidenced by the paintings in Spain's Altamira cave and France's Lascaux cave. Examples of fresco paintings using similar techniques exist on the walls in Herculaneum and in Pompeii, but at best they were precursors of the Renaissance. The advanced art of the Renaissance fresco was created by Masaccio, whose early-fifteenth-century frescos for the Brancacci Chapel of the convent church of Santa Maria del Carmine in Florence inspired all the great painters who followed him, from Ghirlandaio to da Vinci to Michelangelo Buonarroti. The Renaissance critic Vasari observed that the technique was widely used by the ancients, but that Masaccio's approach was the apex of that ancient tradition.[7]

The word "*fresco*" means "fresh," referring to wet plaster (*calcina*) before it dries. There were two kinds of fresco—*buon' fresco* (or good or true fresco) which is essentially moist fresco, and *fresco secco* (or dry fresco), in which the colors are applied after the plaster has dried and the pigments are mixed with a glue or casein base. In a sense, *fresco secco* is not unlike oil painting and has some of the same limitations. The great advantage of *buon' fresco* is that the pigments become part of the plaster and therefore part of the wall, rather than being laid on top of the wall as with *fresco secco.* The lime that is in the plaster becomes the binding agent in *buon' fresco.* As the lime dries, it turns to calcium carbonate that soaks up the pigments and incorporates the colors into the plaster. The colors were usually derived directly from the earth, from minerals such as cinnabar and black and red hematite.

The preparation of the wall for fresco painting is nearly as complex and difficult as the painting itself. If the wall has not been prepared properly, it might crack after the colors have been applied and either tarnish the beauty of the fresco or destroy it all together. Fresco painting requires six layers of underlying plaster, or stucco, all applied with a rule and plummet, to be a reliable surface for the artist. The first three are made up of a combination of lime and powdered brick that has been ground finely. The Greeks used to make large batches of this stucco, pounding it with a kind of oversized mortar and pestle until the lime and the brick were ground so finely and mixed so thoroughly that when mixed with water it would create a kind of viscous mud. The lime was the chief ingredient in this mixture, and it often was necessary to age the lime by soaking it in water for at least three years in order to prevent cracking, and had to be burnt in a kiln in order to bring out its brilliant white color. At one time in Venice, it was illegal to use lime that was less than three years old because it would produce shoddy work. Once the wall had been prepared for plastering, the artisans smoothed on the mixture of lime and powdered brick, or in the case of Roman artists, *pozzolana,* or volcanic ash, and waited for the mixture to dry thoroughly. A second coat was then spread on top of the first, and the artisans took time off to let it dry before they spread a third coat. Lots of time was spent sitting around waiting for things to dry.

The next stage was to put on three coats of the lime mixed with marble dust. The first layer, the *rinzafatto,* was relatively thick, and when it dried, the workmen would spread the second layer, the *arriccio* or *arricciato,* which had to be thinner than the first, on top of that. Finally, when that dried, they would spread the last layer, the *intonaco,* onto the wall and this had to be the thinnest coat of all.

After the six coats dried, the top coat would be polished with a piece of smooth wood, which gave the surface a smooth white luster. The colors applied by the artist would not fade if applied properly, because the moisture evaporated by the lime would leave behind a porous crystalline structure that would in turn absorb the colors and incorporate them into the calcium carbonate that formed as the plaster dried. The wall could be easily cleaned if soiled, and the colors would not fade or change with age. You cannot rub them off without destroying the plaster, and the painting resists the ravages of time. No wonder Michelangelo would not paint in oils when fresco, especially when cleaned and restored, would be found to last for centuries. In 1999, the *Last Judgment* underwent just such a restoration, and the fresco seemed to come alive once again—the resurrection of a resurrection.

While he was painting the Sistine Chapel ceiling frescos, Michelangelo had learned the hard way about the proper preparation for fresco and how local materials can change everything. When he started the work, he brought some of the best fresco painters from Florence to Rome to work for him, but he became dissatisfied with their work, dismissed them all, destroyed what they had done, and began to work alone. He wanted to have complete control over the project. He ordered the natural pigments himself and had them sent to him from Florence. Then he ground the colors himself, refusing to trust anyone else to assist him. But he did not understand the difference between Florentine marble and Roman travertine when ground into dust and used in lime. A third of the way through the project, he ran into a serious problem because of his ignorance of the crucial difference. During the winter, while the north wind was blowing, the plaster he was using began to turn moldy. What he didn't know was that the Roman plaster was mixed with *pozzolana,* which darkens the white lime. When the mixture is wet, it effloresces, unlike marble, which is generally harder than travertine and less porous.

While marble is a metamorphic rock produced from limestone under heat and pressure, travertine is a sedimentary rock, precipitated from either hot or cold springs, in which the water becomes saturated with calcium bicarbonate from limestone and then bubbles some of the carbon dioxide into the atmosphere, like fizzy water. When that happens, it recrystallizes to calcite, encrusting biotic debris, which only accelerates the process. Travertine is capable of holding more water in its structure and therefore takes longer to dry. Because the plaster remained wet longer, it would grow mold on its surface with time. When Michelangelo explained this problem to Pope Julius, the pope sent him to Giuliano da San Gallo, a Florentine architect who taught Michelangelo how to get rid of the mold.[8]

Painting in fresco is the inverse of the spontaneous painting of a modern artist. Conceivably, a contemporary artist could take a squirt gun and spray wet plaster with color and produce something like a fresco, but the mindset of the Renaissance painters was completely different. Fresco requires hours of preparation and conceptualization until every figure, every position, every shadow is clear in the mind of the artist. There is nothing spontaneous about it, at least not as it was practiced in the Renaissance. The larger and more complex the fresco, the greater the preparation. Michelangelo's technique was to begin with a series of hurried drawings that laid out the general concept. First of all, he would experiment with the structure of the painting, with the relationships of the individual groups, trying to see the entire work as if it were already completed. These drawings would become more specific with each attempt, until the concept had begun to gel. Michelangelo probably began this process before the death of Pope Clement, soon after their meeting in the bishop's garden at San Miniato al Tedesco, but it had not progressed very far. From these conversations, Michelangelo took his initial concept and now developed them into a second phase, to flesh out the dramatis personae who would be on stage at the end of time.[9]

Michelangelo created clay models of each of the figures so that he could see them in three dimensions. Holding a candle at various points around each model, he studied how the light fell upon the figure and the shape of the shadows cast by that light. By moving the candle closer and farther from the model he created different types of light, from sharp, hard light with deep shadows to soft ambient light casting bare, almost ghostly shadows. Using the drawings and the models, Michelangelo presented his ideas in a visible form, first to Pope Clement and then to Pope Paul, so they could see the concept for themselves.

The insult perceived by Michelangelo regarding Sebastiano's preparation of the wall for oil paints is rooted in the difference between fresco painting and oil painting. Once the wall is prepared the fresco painter must spread just enough fresh plaster on the wall each day that can be painted in that day. The sections of plaster are called *giornata,* and the painting must be finished on each *giornate* by the end of the day, or the artist must scrape that day's work off and start over. Vasari points out in his book on technique that fresco painting requires a dexterous, sure, and resolute hand, and impeccable judgment.[10] The artist must understand the properties of each color and how it changes with time, because the color may look one way on wet plaster and another way on dry. There's no room for doodling in fresco, because once the plaster dries, it can be changed only by chiseling it off and starting again.

What's more, the form doesn't allow for the artist to change his mind mid-painting because once the colors have been applied, they cannot be easily changed. One can paint over mistakes *a secco,* but that correction is less permanent than the original and the correction would be visible. The artist has to get it right the first time, which means that he must have prepared diligently before setting color to the wall, and must have a sharp concept of what he wants to do before doing it. If there is any delay in painting, the plaster forms a thin crust that will all too easily grow mold, in all kinds of weather, from the cold or heat or wet air.[11] The plaster must be kept moist or the colors will not penetrate. The colors must also be made from earth, not metals, because earth colors last while metals are subject to color change with time and weather. The white must be made of calcined travertine, which produces the purest whites, called *bianco Sangiovanni.* Ordinary white pigment, made from lead, cannot be used in fresco.

Each area must be completed in a day. Michelangelo had discovered the difficulties and limitations of this art form while he was painting the Sistine Chapel ceiling. He had already learned the art of *buon' fresco* under Ghirlandaio, one of the great fresco painters of Florence, but he had never thought of himself as accomplished in the art until he finished the ceiling. First and foremost he was a sculptor after all. The *Last Judgment,* however, was to be painted using all of his experience—it was the summation of all his training.

Sebastiano's assumption of Michelangelo's artistic control of the *Last Judgment* when he ordered the wall prepared for oil painting was an insult. Michelangelo felt that both the pope and Sebastiano had misjudged him, that by usurping his artistic decision, they thought him incapable of the rigors of fresco painting. He saw Sebastiano as a lazy artist, who took the easy way rather than the best way. He would show them that he had lost none of the vigor of his youth, or not that much anyway. He was Michelangelo Buonarroti, and he would paint for the ages, not just for the moment. The pope simply wanted "something from Michelangelo" and Sebastiano wanted to turn him into his own artistic creature.

Michelangelo would have none of it. He insisted that the preparation set in place by Sebastiano be chiseled away and the wall prepared for *buon' fresco.* This would take nearly a year to complete, but Michelangelo insisted on it nevertheless.

It is possible that Michelangelo had waited all those months to speak up because he hadn't yet warmed to the fresco project. The commission still seemed like something forced upon him, a vision that was not his own, which had happened all too often in his dealings with powerful popes.

After his dispute with Sebastiano, Michelangelo retreated into himself and told everyone how badly he had been treated by his old friend. By this time, the pope had taken the hint that his official court artist and architect would not be budged on this matter, and that he would only paint the *Last Judgment* in a traditional fresco process.

CHAPTER FIVE

Colors

The standard architectural structure for churches and chapels in the Catholic Church is to place the altar wall on the eastern side of the building so that Mass can be said as the sun rises, just as Jesus rose from the tomb. Given its position within the Vatican buildings, the builders of the Sistine Chapel were obliged to put the altar wall on the west wall, the direction of the setting sun, the direction of death. The architect who originally designed the chapel for Pope Sixtus IV (the uncle of Julius II who originally commissioned

Michelangelo to paint the vaulted ceiling) created it to fit the dimensions of the Temple of Solomon, found in 1 Kings 6:2.[1] Accordingly, the Sistine Chapel was built 60 cubits (about 18 inches) long, twenty wide, and twenty-five high.

Pope Sixtus IV designed the chapel to serve as the *Capella Papalis*, the chapel for the papal court, namely the pope with his top advisers and the members of his ecclesiastical administration or the Curia. Although the mood of Michelangelo's *Last Judgment* would seem appropriate for a funerary chapel, it would not appear so in a palace chapel like the Sistine. However, because of the odd placement of the chapel itself, the result seems particularly harmonious. The fresco seems appropriate for that western wall and the setting sun because it depicts the end of the world. This is the great catastrophe, the death of this universe, in which all the actions and thoughts of the human race are summed up in the division between the elect and the damned.

About a year into the project, Michelangelo warmed to his subject. At his age, the reality of death was ever present on his mind, and he took solace in the fact that he had been a loyal son of the church. He had disagreed with the popes he had served, often at a profound level, because his faith was fairly straightforward while their faith was often a Gordian knot of faith, family obligations, and politics. He thought his faith in the church was often stronger than theirs. No matter what his sins were, however, he knew they could be forgiven by the actions of the same church that had told him they were sins in the first place.

Mixed with that sense of the nearness of his death was the sense that the world itself was changing and the church was caught between its love for tradition and its need to be ready for the future. The Protestant Reformation had taken the lead and the Catholic Reformation was like a reluctant horse that refused to leave the gate. But with the sack of Rome ten years earlier, all that started to change. Michelangelo wanted to be a part of that change, for he could see evidence all around the city of Rome of how the church had corrupted itself. But he also wanted to remain loyal to the institution that allowed him to work—the church was his home.[2] His allegiance could have been summed up in Peter's words to Jesus: "To whom shall we go? You have the words of eternal life." (John 6:68)[3] Because Michelangelo was so deeply Catholic, he was sure that the church would survive the change and renew itself through reform.

The *Last Judgment,* then, had slowly transformed from an annoyance to the project of the day. New ideas came to him, new thoughts about fresco painting, new notions about theology in general, and the theology of the Catholic Reformation in particular. It would be a huge painting, far greater in many ways than his famous ceiling, which was painted as a series of panels, that each told its own story. The *Last Judgment* would be a single dramatic work. The fresco would measure 46 feet by 43 feet, an area of 1,978 square feet. To make this preparation, Michelangelo ordered two windows to be walled up, the coat of arms of Pope Sixtus IV della Rovere just below his own figure of Jonah to be removed, and the corbel beneath the coat of arms to be reduced in size.

The preparation was complicated by the presence of older frescos. In 1482, three fresco painters, Pietro Perugino, Sandro Botticelli, and Domenico Ghirlandaio had completed a series of frescos along the side walls of the Sistine Chapel, just after it was rebuilt and reopened by Pope Sixtus IV. These panels depicted the life of Moses on one side, and the life of Christ, the new Moses, on the other. Above these, they painted a series of portraits of important popes and below, they painted trompe l'oeil draperies. Perugino had also added an altar piece, showing the Assumption of the Virgin with Pope Sixtus IV kneeling before her, but this had been damaged in a fire.[4] At first, Michelangelo wanted to preserve this altar piece as well as the two lunettes of his own, but after a while, his concept for the *Last Judgment* changed to include the entire wall, and so he ordered the workmen to destroy all of these earlier works, including his own.

Destroying Perugino's frescos on the altar wall was no big deal for Michelangelo. In 1500, when Michelangelo was still a young artist on the rise in Florence, he had met the artist who, after seeing his most recent work (and probably envious of the brilliance of the younger artist) damned the work with faint praise and sly innuendo. Michelangelo responded in kind, calling Perugino a "bungler in art"

in public. Perugino tried to sue Michelangelo for defamation of character, but failed.[5]

Michelangelo showed little remorse when destroying these
earlier frescos also because they had been damaged when a fire
broke out in the draperies near the wall. Perugino's frescos—his
Assumption and Coronation of the Virgin, the *Finding of Moses* on the
left side of the wall, and the *Birth of Christ* on the right side were
destroyed. What mattered to Michelangelo was the work at hand,
not the work of the past.

Michelangelo also ordered the destruction of frescos depicting the
first four popes—Jesus, Peter, Linus, and Cletus—which had been
painted into virtual niches flanking the windows that he ordered
bricked up—and he took over the space that had been reserved for
two tapestries that had been designed by Raphael, commissioned by
Pope Leo X, and woven in Brussels in 1520. The first of six tapestries
depicted the life of St. Paul, while the second illustrated the life of
St. Peter.

What was most difficult for Michelangelo, however, was his decision to destroy pieces of his own ceiling fresco, two lunettes painted in
1512 showing the ancestors of Christ, with Abraham, Isaac, Jacob, and
Judah on the left lunette, and Phares, Esron, and Aram on the right.
His earlier drawings indicate that he tried to save them but eventually
gave up. One of the drawings, the second of only two in existence—
the first is at the Royal Museum at Windsor Castle and the latter at the
Casa Buonarroti in Florence—shows a fairly late design for the *Last
Judgment* that still includes the older lunettes. But a new idea, or the
expansion of an old idea actually, had come to him between the time
he drew that sketch and the time he began the fresco and his lunettes
were destroyed.

Most Renaissance paintings included a frame to create a limited space,
a window through which the viewer could enter the painting. For

theological reasons and possibly based upon the cosmology of Nicholas of Cusa, the Catholic bishop of Brixen, Germany, who in the previous century had denied the finiteness of the universe, Michelangelo designed the *Last Judgment* to stretch from wall to wall without a frame, creating an implied infinite space, as if the wall had disappeared and the viewer was participating in the Day of Judgment. This had the effect of drawing the viewer into the scene, causing them to question their own lives and their own place on that terrible day. This effect brings to mind scenes from Dante, matched with lines from the thirteenth-century *Dies Irae*—the hymn sung on All Souls' Day and after communion at every funeral.

> The day of wrath, that day
> when the world will burn to ashes
> as prophesied by David and the Sybil.
>
> What terror there will be
> when the Lord will come
> to judge all righteously![6]

The new fresco would exist as an autonomous artistic and spiritual unit, an entity, a creature that would stand apart from the predated iconography of the chapel. It was meant to astound the beholder, a thing in itself, keyed to neither the existing frescos on the lateral walls nor to Michelangelo's ceiling. It was not coordinated with them in any way—the characters were on a completely different scale, almost inhuman in their exaggerated musculature, like superheroes twisting in the air. Michelangelo chose the colors for this fresco without regard to creating a harmony with the colors he had used for his ceiling. He rejected the rich spectrum of colors he had used decades before, employing instead only two dominant colors—a warm flesh color (an accommodation of grays and browns) for the naked bodies and a cool blue mixed with azurite for the skies. To create the skies, he ordered a light underpainting of white shading into an almost transparent red to give the final ultramarine color an increasing depth and sense of distance.

In planning his design, Michelangelo understood that the primary beholder for this fresco would be the pope and not the public at large. Therefore, he set the structure of the fresco so that its proper viewing points would correspond with the places that the pope would inhabit in the chapel. The first of these was the papal throne just below the prophet Jeremiah, before the second pilaster of the left wall. While the pope could see the entire fresco from this point, the full power of it was turned away from him.

The real power of the fresco was turned toward the second view-point. This was a small window located in the first bay of the right lateral wall. This window led to a secret chamber that had been built by Julius II so the reigning pope could view the mass without being seen. The room has since been walled up, but the window remains. It was to this viewpoint that Michelangelo oriented the full impact of the fresco. Through this window, the pope could see Christ turned toward him. From here, the all-powerful son of God would catch his eye and the tragedy of each figure behind Christ, from the martyrs and saints to the damned, would best be displayed. The pope, whoever he might be in the future, would receive the full impact of the message. Beware, Christ seems to admonish, and be the good shepherd or suffer the consequences. From this viewpoint, the fresco is most clearly a reformer's message to the visible head of the church. Like Dante, Michelangelo was ready to consign luxurious popes, warrior popes, and ambitious popes to the infernal regions of the universe.

Beyond this, the fresco would be structured as a series of groups, each working out a specific drama, with the entire cacophonous moment frozen in timelessness to shock and awe the beholder. As in his sculptures, Michelangelo imparted a sense in the fresco that the figures had not been painted onto the surface of the wall but had been coaxed out of the substance of the plaster, freed from stone and mortar to stand outside, in this world, alive. The central axis of the fresco starts beneath the corbel, with groups of figures depicted nearly symmetrically on both sides. For each major figure on one side, there is another on the other side, so that the impressive Christ, dominating the scene is surrounded by voices crying out for justice and for salvation, by the praise of the saints and the rage of the damned.

Unlike medieval Last Judgment scenes, there are no obvious hierarchical zones, going from top to bottom, from angels to saints, to the
living, to those in purgatory, to the damned. In Michelangelo's fresco,
the characters are divided into groups that flow into each other so that
the piece forms a dramatic unit. This novel conception is no longer
about reasserting social structure but about encoding a dynamic new
pattern, with the sun and God in the form of Christ at the center. The
masses of naked figures swirl around as if drawn by a mystical force—a
force that we would call gravity today. The figures are divided into two
fairly distinct orbital circles, those who are closest to Christ are there
through some greatness of action, either great in sanctity or great in
damnation, and those who are placed farther away from the central
Christ figure. The great mass of humanity is here, where each character seeks their proper place defined by their faith or lack of it and
by their deeds, good or evil.[7] In this swirling moment, it is the church
that unites all into one body, good or evil notwithstanding.

Michelangelo's fresco would not take place in this world, but in
a mythic world, as if on another planet with strange blue green skies.
From the time of the early Renaissance, knowledge of the heavens
had been growing at an alarming pace. From a tidy little earth-cen-
tered system limited by crystalline spheres, it had become an infinite
space, filled with stars and planets. This idea had become current
among the intelligentsia long before Copernicus was born. Certainly,
Michelangelo had heard Nicholas of Cusa and probably knew something of his philosophical ideas, because he had become a major voice
in Neoplatonic circles.

Michelangelo's new idea was to create a sense of infinite space
as described by Cusanus, so that the Last Judgment would not take
place inside a box but would stretch out beyond earth, beyond the
solar system, and embrace all the stars. The entire universe would be
judged on that day, a truly terrible day. He had tried to encompass the
universe in a limited way in the ceiling, by laying out salvation history,
which is within time, and not outside of time, as is the Last Judgment.
However, since the vault did not depict a single dramatic event, the
effect is largely lost. In the *Last Judgment*, the power of Christ reaches
out to the infinite universe and even the heavens obey.

The moment depicted is the exact moment of judgment, when every soul is poised to hear its doom. Universal anxiety twists each soul—the elect straining for the sky, helped by the muscular arms of angels. On each face is the terrible insecurity of one awaiting the fall of the dice, the moment of summation of the person's entire life. The damned begin to realize the awful truth as they fall back to earth, heavy with their fleshly sins, dragged downward by legions of demons and pummeled from above by angels. As they fall, they shrink in size, a matter of perspective that has as much to do with the shape of the wall as with the size of the figures.

The new wall preparation was unlike any other. The wall originally sloped backward, with the top about 5½ inches farther back than the bottom. Michelangelo wanted to create a unique effect with this fresco by structurally altering the wall to slope forward slightly. There would be a looming effect on the viewer, who would feel as if the judgment were falling upon him. He ordered the workmen to chisel the masonry back 5⅞ inches at the top, and as they moved downward, to chisel gradually deeper and deeper into the wall until the bottom was 23⅛ inches farther back from its original place. They then took specially fired bricks, each 5⅞ inches thick, and refaced the wall to Michelangelo's specifications.

When they were done, the top of the wall overhung the bottom by 11¾ inches, so that one could see the forward inclination from the ground. Michelangelo wanted to create a visual effect not unlike the swelling of a classical column. Entasis in architecture is an ancient technique that substitutes a convex surface for a flat surface in order to correct an optical illusion that makes cylindrical columns appear pinched and flat surfaces appear convex. Because of his desire to create an optical effect through the wall preparation, Michelangelo took a great deal of time checking and rechecking the foreshortened figures, and making corrections to their position in ways that he had not done with the ceiling fresco.

Altogether, Michelangelo ordered 81 cubic yards of the masonry removed. Giorgio Vasari thought that this was done in order to keep dust and grime—especially the smoke from burning candles—from collecting on the fresco surface. But an inclined surface like this gets dirty faster since the smoke collects on it more directly. Only two years after the unveiling of the *Last Judgment,* Pope Paul III had to create the position of "fresco cleaner" in order to keep Michelangelo's work from disappearing in the grime.

In 1511, when he was working on the ceiling, Michelangelo was acting as a subcontractor. Pope Julius had provided him with a set amount of money and he was expected to pay for all of his equipment, the pigments, the preparation of the wall, his assistants, and even the scaffolding out of that money. Because he made his own arrangements, he made certain to buy most of his pigments from his fellow Florentines and not from Venice, their chief rival in the pigment business.

There were forty painter's workshops in Florence that supported a thriving business in colors and paints and an equally successful business in Venice. Most of this Florentine business was operated in local monasteries, most notably the Gesuati friars, who were famous for their colors. But artists could also order their pigments from local apothecaries and even physicians, because the artists were members of the *Arte dei Speziali e Medici* (the Guild of Apothecaries and Doctors) since most of the colors and fixatives that they used could also be used as medicines. Doctors often prescribed gum tragacanth for coughs, laryngitis, and sores on the eyelids, but it was also mixed with water to suspend pigments. The root of the madder plant was used in making red lake, an important red pigment, but it was also employed as a cure for sciatica. Darío Varatori, an artist from Padua was once under the care of a physician, who gave him medicine to take for his condition. Varatori opened the bottle, sniffed the medicine, dipped his brush into the bottle and brushed the solution onto the wall. Both the wall and the artist survived.[8]

But when he ordered the pigments for the *Last Judgment* on May 18, 1536, Michelangelo's financial fortunes had changed. Because

Paul III had named him to the position of papal artist and architect, all expenses were paid by the Vatican, and the Vatican, in the person of Jacopo Meleghino, the pope's commissioner of papal shops, did the ordering. At first, he ordered the colors from Venice, but later switched them to Ferrara, his native city. Meleghino kept meticulous records—much better records than Michelangelo kept when he had painted the ceiling—writing down each payment, the cost of the pigments, and the place they were purchased for his accounting to the pope. Sadly, the only pigments that he noted by color in his account book were those for various shades of blue, since those pigments were the most difficult to attain and the most expensive. Pigments for the other colors—red, green, yellow, ocher—could easily be manufactured from common minerals such as cinnabar, but most blue colors came from vegetable dyes that did not last as long and quickly turned a sickly green.

For the *Last Judgment,* Michelangelo spared no expense because the expense wasn't his. Most notable were his large orders of ultramarine, the green-blue.[9] This was probably the most expensive pigment available because it was made from a semiprecious mineral, lapis lazuli. The only other blue color he purchased was the deep blue made from azurite. On November 21, Meleghino ordered "10 pounds of German blue" or azurite from Ferrara, probably to be mixed with ultramarine to create various shades of sky.[10]

Lapis lazuli had been sold quite widely in the Middle East from civilization's earliest times. Ornamental objects using lapis appeared in Iran, Mesopotamia, and the Russian steppes, and jewelry and other objects have been found in Egypt dating back to 3500 BCE. Sources of lapis lazuli dotted Central Asia all the way to Burma, stretching back to prehistoric times. Lapis was traded in Italy, and caravans carried objects made of the semiprecious stone from Europe to India over centuries. Lapis lazuli was first used as a pigment in Afghan rock paintings dating back to the sixth or seventh century CE. By the seventh century the pigment began to move west, gradually replacing Egyptian blue. But the expense of the mineral never diminished, and its use as a fresco pigment was rare for that reason. No one really quite knows the provenance for Michelangelo's ultramarine. One possible site was at Sar-e-Sang, located in Budakhshan, Afghanistan. Many assumed that this was the most likely site until the recent restoration of the *Last Judgment* produced a series of mineralogical studies showing that the chemical content of Michelangelo's pigment did not match that from Afghanistan. The other possibility for the source of lapis lazuli was the area around Castelli Romani and Mount Vesuvius. While this site seems more likely given its proximity to Rome, the scarcity of the outcroppings casts doubt on this site as well.

Natural ultramarine was not only a rare and expensive pigment, it was also difficult to use and not good for fresco. To vary the tones of the sky, Michelangelo had to paint partly in ultramarine and partly in tempera, a technique in which pigments are mixed with egg yolk. The egg mixture dries quickly and sticks tenaciously to whatever surface it is applied. Honey, water, and milk in the form of casein, along with large amounts of plant gums, are sometimes added to the mix for texture. Tempera was an old technique that predated *buon' fresco* and was chiefly used for panel painting in the ancient and medieval world, along with encaustic, which was painting with hot wax mixed with pigments. The use of tempera allowed Michelangelo to fine tune his sky, which became the most striking aspect of his new fresco. Beyond the ultramarine, however, most of the colors used in the *Last Judgment* were the same as he used in the ceiling, though they were ordered from different sources.

Meanwhile, the workmen lathered on the *arriccio* (the second plaster coat), this time for fresco, and Michelangelo kept busy preparing the cartoons for each of the figures. By the time the *intonaco* had been smoothed onto the *arriccio*, the cartoons were complete, along with several smaller drawings and studies. The *arriccio* on this fresco was quite thin, never more than seven millimeters thick, while the *intonaco* was about four millimeters. The workmen mixed the mortar from a combination of *pozzolana*, the volcanic ash found commonly in southern Italy, and lime, in a proportion of three measures of ash to one of lime. The lime, which was often a mixture of lime and ground marble dust, had to soak in water for at least six months and be stirred regularly, until it formed a white sludge. In Venice, it was against the law to use lime that had been soaked for less than three years, because to do so would be to use inferior lime that would likely crumble, like using inferior mortar in a stone building.[11] This aged sludge would then be mixed with sand. The *pozzolana* used in Rome had grains that were often irregular in size and shape, and the mixture had to be pounded with a mortar and pestle to smooth it out. In places where the artist needed an especially smooth surface, his assistants could use sand along with the volcanic ash. This would smooth out the mortar to create a more compact surface. Sand would lighten the mortar as well, reflecting the light in striking ways. The workmen smoothed and pressed the *intonaco* into a tight, compact surface that was free of gaps, bubbles, or bumps.

Michelangelo officially began the fresco when he ordered the scaffolding erected early in 1536. By that summer, he climbed the scaffolding to paint the first *giornate*, or section of the fresco that could be painted in one day, in the lunette on the upper left. Generally, he worked in boustrophedon fashion, as an oxen plows a field, back and forth, from the left to the right, and then down one row, then back to the left again. Sometimes, he would stop to alter *a secco* a figure already painted, mainly to revise the foreshortening of figures, or to change the placement of a hand or foot.

His servant Urbino spent most of the time grinding pigments, which would then be mixed with water for painting onto the wet plaster. For this, Urbino was paid four scudi a month, with sixty ducats given to him by Pope Paul as a tip when the fresco was completed. Urbino—Amadore Francesco d'Urbino—had been both a student and assistant of the master Michelangelo since 1530, replacing Antonio Mini, who had been Michelangelo's trusted student for decades, and Michelangelo cared for Urbino as he had cared for Mini. Urbino helped from time to time with the cartoons, and a careful eye can see his work by the noticeable drop in the quality of detail and expression. For the ceiling, Michelangelo had employed a team of fresco artists from Florence but he soon quarreled with them and sent them packing, preferring to do the work himself. By this time, he had learned his lesson and allowed only Urbino to accompany him up the scaffold to prepare the plaster and grind the colors. On November 18, 1545, the pope named Urbino *mundator picturarum capellarum palatii,* or the "fresco cleaner" for the Sistine Chapel, a permanent position with its own salary.

In 1555, when Urbino died, Michelangelo became the executor of his will and arranged for the care of his two sons and his wife. Michelangelo later sketched pictures of her two sons, which were admired by the Duke of Urbino, and their mother was "advised" to hand the sketches over to the duke as a gift. She did so, but she asked Michelangelo if another painter could make copies of the sketches for her. This was done and they were given to her, but she never saw the original sketches again.

In September 1537, Michelangelo received a strange letter from one of the most notorious satirists of the age, Pietro Aretino. Aretino wasn't called the "scourge of princes" for nothing. He was not just a satirist, but a blackmailer and a pornographer. His writings today are categorized under "erotica" and are probably the main reason he is still remembered. Michelangelo's old friend Berni, another satirist, couldn't stand Aretino and traded literary insults with him on a regular basis, penning a long poem in which he prophesied that one day Aretino would be hanged.

Pietro Aretino was born a bastard in Arezzo—thus the name Aretino ("from Arezzo")—and spent his youth in Perugia, where he gathered whatever education he could. He entered the public sphere when he published a mock last will and testament for Pope Leo X's pet elephant, named Hanno, who had recently died. In it, Hanno wills his testicles to a cardinal who was famous for his philandering. The fact that Pope Clement patronized him says more about the Renaissance mindset than the morals of the Pope. Clement, who was open-minded to a fault, was a greater lover of art than he was of religion. He had a coarse sense of humor, and Aretino's pornographic sonnets would have appealed to him. Had Aretino appeared at the papal court later, during the Catholic Reformation, he would have been arrested.

Aretino stayed in Rome for a time, until his lampoons offended so many people, most especially Cardinal Gilberti, who was prominent in the Catholic Reform movement. Gilberti was so incensed that his agents threatened Aretino's life on several occasions and attempted to assassinate him at least once. Aretino fled Rome and ended up in the most antipapal city in Italy—Venice—where he was received as a conquering hero and became the bosom friend of Titian, Michelangelo's chief living rival in artistic greatness.

Michelangelo understood from the beginning that the letter he received from Aretino was dangerous and that Aretino could and probably would make his life miserable if he wasn't treated correctly, and maybe even if he was.[12] It was a presumptuous letter, giving Michelangelo directions on how this new fresco of his should look. Only Aretino would have had the ego to attempt this approach with Michelangelo because Aretino was used to holding all of Italy in terror of his pen.

> Who would not be petrified to set his brush to so intimidating a subject? There, the Antichrist encircled by a horde of souls, with such a look about him that only one like you could imagine it. There, terror on the faces of the living...on seeing this vision of ruin on the Day of Judgment, my thoughts impel me to exclaim, "if we suffer such fear and trembling while contemplating this work of Buonarroti, then how much greater will be our suffering when we are judged by the One who must judge us. [13]

Michelangelo had good reason to be cautious when he received this letter. Aretino had the reputation of a vengeful nature, capable of lashing out with ten times the force of what he had received. He didn't want to dawdle. Quickly, he sent back a good-humored reply.

> When I received your letter, I felt boy joy and sadness together. On one hand, I rejoiced that the letter came from you, since you are so

gifted among us all. On the other hand, I grieve terribly, because
I had already completed much of the composition, and therefore
cannot use what you have imagined in the fresco, even though your
description is such that if the Judgment Day had already happened,
and you had seen it with your own eyes, your words could not have
pictured it better.[14]

Perhaps Michelangelo understood better than most what was about
to happen to him. Perhaps he understood that no matter what he did
from this point on, he would suffer for it.

CHAPTER SIX

The Children of Savonarola

For almost a year and a half after he had arrived in Rome, Michelangelo had sat in his house on the Macel de Corvi and brooded over the new commission for the *Last Judgment*. He had entered the stage of life when making a good death becomes more important, and as with everything else he did, he became obsessed with it. He feared death, of course, but most of all he feared what came after.

The Macel de Corvi, where Michelangelo's house was located, was never a main thoroughfare, just a narrow track between rows of houses. The street no longer exists in contemporary Rome because it was destroyed in the twentieth century by construction for the monument to Victor Emmanuel. The façade of the house was moved and built into a wall for a reservoir on the Janiculum. The house was located in the old medieval section of the city, on a street just off a piazza and across the street from a church. There is an old woodcut that shows the piazza with little shops on both sides, a peasant carrying a sack of wheat, and people standing in the middle of the avenue in little groups, as Romans often do, exchanging the news of the day, while important people ride by in carriages, aloof from the common herd. The houses on both sides have four stories, shops on the first floor and terra cotta roof tiles on top. The windows are narrow and rectangular, with shutters to deflect the noise of the street and to insulate the rooms from the heat of summer and the cold winds of winter. The tomb of Caio Publicio Bibulo, "the people's builder," which had once stood outside the walls of the ancient city and marks the beginning of via Flaminia, one of the oldest Roman consular roads, is near the north side of the piazza, and is still there.

Michelangelo's house was similar to the others, but with only two floors, arched windows, and doors on the first floor. In addition to his beloved servant Urbino, his new salary as artist and architect to the papal court allowed him to have a small group of servants who took care of the business of the house. The property included two small cottages and a fair amount of land, which was hard to come by in Rome even then. But even if his lodging had improved greatly in the twenty-eight years since his painting of the Sistine Chapel ceiling, his habits had not. At sixty-four, Michelangelo ate sparingly and lived a solitary life. He was still possessed by his need to work; his creative fires were still burning, and partly for religious reasons, he would not allow himself the luxuries claimed by the aristocracy and the hierarchy. His clothes were simple wool and linen, and he refused to dress in brocades. He never owned a carriage, and moved about Rome on foot, and rode a horse or a mule in the country. While he enjoyed the company of his friends, he never entertained them with banquets or made obvious displays of wealth.

He worked himself to exhaustion and often fell asleep in his clothes, stinking from body odor. Sometimes he wore the same set of clothes, too long without changing them. His exhaustion led to moodiness and his questionable hygiene kept people away, and several times nearly destroyed his health. He was still cheeky with popes, often wearing an old felt hat when visiting with Pope Paul and not taking it off. It was a mark of the regard Paul III had for him that he never chided him about it, as Clement would have.

A report in the *Journal of Medical Biography* recently argued that Michelangelo suffered from Asperger's syndrome, a high-functioning form of autism that affects the way people process information but does not affect the person's native intelligence.[1] People with Asperger's have deficiencies in social skills, obsessive routines, and difficulty reading body language, and are so naïve about the true feelings and intentions of others that it makes them paranoid and reactive to insults, real or imagined. They are often overly sensitive to sounds, smells, tastes, and sights, and sometimes display amazing abilities in one area or other. Most people who meet them think of them as odd, eccentric, perhaps brilliantly so, but unusual nevertheless.

The report claims that Michelangelo's single-minded attention to work, his obsessions over money and family, his erratic behavior, and his inability to form healthy attachments are solid evidence for this condition. His assistants often remarked that he was "strange and obsessed" when he worked, and that he kept a vigilance over their work that exhausted everyone. On his deathbed, when his nephew Lionardo came from Florence to see him, he would not receive him, saying that the nephew had only come to ensure that his inheritance was secure. He had a short temper, was sarcastic, and often walked away from a conversation in the middle of a sentence, or suddenly distanced himself from long-term friends and allies. His break with Sebastiano del Piombo is an obvious case in point. Whether his grumbling silence was a symptom of Asperger's, however, or just passive-aggressive behavior is uncertain. Criticism, earned or unearned, drove him into terrible depressions, and when threatened, he often left whatever city he lived in during the night and hid, turning up in Carrara or Venice or Bologna.

Moreover, as he prepared himself for executing the *Last Judgment,* Michelangelo was still suffering the effects of the terrible depression that had gripped him in his last days in Florence. The melancholy style of the male figure representing *Day* and the female figure representing *Night* that he sculpted for the Medici Chapel in the Church of San Lorenzo in Florence expressed what he felt even while he was in Rome—that time leads inevitably to death, a process that not even fame can prevent.[2] He could feel his own powers waning. In a letter to Francesco Berni, the Florentine satirist and Aretino's nemesis, he complained about a multitude of ailments, from bad vision and deafness to dysuria and diarrhea. He claimed to have syphilis and gout, gallstones and lumbago, bad breath, snoring, and hernia. He obsessed about old age, saying that oak trees and rocks are immortal, but geniuses die.

In many ways, the *Last Judgment* was the perfect project to express his feelings at this stage of his life. He could see that all he knew of the Renaissance was dying, and that the reform that he longed for was leading to a new church with new rules. He was a dedicated republican and hated dictators, but dictators seemed to be a feature of the Italian identity. Deeply disappointed in the state of the world and devoutly Catholic, his primary concern was a happy death. At his age, while he still felt the pains of love, they had receded into second position. He had decided that death was his only release from love, love that had hounded him from childhood.

Still, he had a reputation as a great conversationalist with his friends and possessed a kind and generous spirit. His integrity over small matters was profound. When he was in his eighties, nearly on his deathbed, he insisted on sending 2 gold scudi to Florence on behalf of one of his hired laborers at St. Peter's, and made sure that the money reached the hands of the young man's mother.[3]

In all his suffering, however, Michelangelo was able to keep his sense of humor. Some might think that geniuses prefer intellectual ripostes, third and fourth level puns, with references to Homer, but this was not the case with Michelangelo, who liked potty jokes.

> I've come to know urine
> and the channel from which is exits, those fools

who wake me too early in the morning
cats, dead animals, singing, or privys.[4]

Michelangelo and Francesco Berni kept up a lively comic exchange, swapping poetry and making fun of people when they could. Berni was known for his crude but terribly funny lampoons of just about everyone. His father Nicoló had worked as a notary for a wealthy Florentine family but was himself quite poor. In 1517, Francesco left Florence for Rome, to work as a letter writer for Cardinal Bibbiena, who eventually died, leaving Francesco out of a job. Worse, when the cardinals elected Pope Adrian VI, a dour man with a monk's asceticism and no sense of humor, Berni's risqué poetry offended the new pope and he had to flee the city. Later, after Adrian's unmourned death by poisoning and after the election of Clement VII, who had a sense of humor, Berni found employment as a clerk in the office of Cardinal Gilberti, a leader of the reform movement, and as a datary, the man responsible for granting benefices, sources of income for priests, and matrimonial dispensations for the new pope. But in this job, he actually had to work, which troubled him, so he ended up taking a job with Cardinal Ippolito de Medici, the cousin of the tyrannical Duke of Tuscany, Alessandro de Medici. In 1536, Berni fell ill and died, rumored to have been poisoned by the duke for refusing in turn to poison the duke's cousin, the cardinal.

Michelangelo treasured friends like Berni, who was not only loyal but who also made him laugh—Rome was not a happy place. The memory of the sack burned in her people for nearly a century. When Michelangelo began the *Last Judgment,* the year was 1535, only eight years after the blood and fire of the invasion. Understandably, the people hated the Holy Roman Emperor, hated the Germans, and especially hated the Spanish. A Spaniard caught alone in the streets took his life in his hands.

The people weren't too fond of Pope Clement either. Even after Clement and the emperor had apparently come to terms, the memory seared the consciousness of Romans. The emperor still refused to pay his soldiers and, therefore, they would not have left Rome or abandoned their quest for booty if it had not been for an outbreak of the plague.

Oddly enough, the Romans owed their freedom to a disease. Such memories fired the desire for reform in the city, as the people walked by the places where the bodies had been piled up and remembered the stench of the dead decaying in the streets, remembered the sound of the mothers weeping for their dead children, thrown from windows by drunken soldiers.

A strange confluence of events whirlpooled through Rome. Calls for reform had led to the denunciation of the excesses of the Renaissance; a new spirituality based on the *devotio moderna* that emphasized a personal rather than an institutional relationship with God had exploded in the city. In truth, the new spirituality had been growing since the fourteenth century, the century of the *Imitation of Christ* by Thomas à Kempis, the *Cloud of Unknowing* by an anonymous author, and also the century of Dante, Boccaccio, and Chaucer. But by the sixteenth century, it had really taken hold. All the new orders—the Jesuits, the Theatines, the Discalced Carmelites—built their spiritual disciplines on that new foundation, as had most of the Protestants. Reform was in the air, a reform that shouted, "Repent in your heart and believe!"

What better expression for the rage and despair of the people of Rome than a fresco showing the end of the world, where the just would be separated from the evildoers for all eternity? Clement knew this and so did Paul III. There is no doubt that while Michelangelo prepared himself for painting the fresco, he felt that rage, and knew that a stately medieval last judgment simply wouldn't do. Last judgment themes had been common in the late middle ages but they were more a statement of social order than a dramatic depiction of the end times. The theme soon disappeared during the more optimistic Renaissance when faith in human destiny ran high. After the slaughter in Rome, the dignity of the human race seemed lost in the blood and filth, and thoughts of judgment squatted inside people's minds. The world was a tumbling affair, wrenching and turning in its agony.

Even while Michelangelo's focus on the human body had not changed—his twisted, muscular characters forever caught in the midst of heroic action—his theology, and therefore his politics, was profoundly supportive of the new reforms. He believed, as did most people at the time, that Rome had earned her suffering because of her years of decadence. Michelangelo's own rage, his own desire, his own suffering vibrated with the people's like a tuning fork held to a crystal glass. Everything he painted into the *Last Judgment* reflects this. "The denunciation of the prophets, the woes of the Apocalypse, the invective of Savonarola, the tragedy of Italian history, the sense of present and indwelling sin storm through and through it."[5]

This is the aesthetic difference between Michelangelo's two frescos. The Renaissance optimism of the ceiling had given way to the dark foreboding of the Catholic Reformation for the altar wall. Blood and fire had come between them, and the dire predictions of reformers, from Savonarola to Luther, had come true. Michelangelo had painted the vaulted ceiling during the last sultry days of the Renaissance. He painted the altar wall during the first freeze of the Counter-Reformation, which was not just a Johnny-come-lately attempt at reform, but was a tidal change, a tsunami in the history of Christianity, a shift from unlimited confidence in the power of human action to a hyperconsciousness of sin and a fear of damnation.

After the sack, the emperor could no longer be ignored, and the kings and princes of Europe intimidated the church. Paul III agreed to call a reform council. As Michelangelo polished his design for the *Last Judgment*, sketching hundreds of studies of hands, faces, body postures, and cloud formations, he listened to the sermons of the reformers and agreed. He was no longer the neophyte fresco artist but was now its master, and this new fresco would both express the theology of reform and be faithful to Catholic doctrine.

Savonarola had not been silenced by his death. The spirit that he began spread across Europe along with ideas of other reformers, and it reappeared in Germany in the Lutheran Reformation. Many of the abuses that Luther condemned in his *95 Theses* had been previously condemned by Savonarola in Florence. In fact, almost everyone in Europe saw what had happened to the Renaissance church—corruption in the church had been a matter of satire from the time of Chaucer to Erasmus. Moreover, the reformist spirit continued in the Catholic Church, finding expression not only among the theologians but among the artists. Michelangelo had long been a fellow traveler with the Catholic reformers and found ways to express this in his art. By the time he began to work on the *Last Judgment,* his incipient faith had caught fire once again. At the heart of the Catholic Reformation was a call for a return to an authentic Christianity, a call to rid the church of the worldliness of the Renaissance popes and their circle of princely cardinals.

Savonarola's spirit had begun to emerge once again after the sack of Rome, in the last days of the papacy of Clement VII and the first days of the papacy of Paul III. Under Pope Paul, the Spirituali, a group of Catholic intellectuals with an eye on reform, began to emerge. Prominent among them was Gasparo Contarini, a child of the Venetian noble house of Contarini. He soon became a successful diplomat in the service of Venice, and those who sat across from him in negotiation often marveled at his reasonable nature and his soft-spoken manner. For five years, from 1520 to 1525, he was Venice's ambassador to the Holy Roman Emperor, Charles V, but he soon found himself caught in a war between the emperor and his native city, which had allied itself with France. In April 1521, he attended the Diet of Worms which was presided over by the emperor, at which Luther declined to recant his teachings, but he didn't encounter Martin Luther while he was there. After the sack of Rome, Contarini took a hand in reconciling the emperor and Pope Clement VII, who then set about laying siege to Florence and chasing down the rebel leaders, including Michelangelo Buonarroti.

Soon after, the doge of Venice sent Contarini to Rome to act as the Venetian representative to the Vatican. In 1535, Pope Paul III named him a cardinal. This was unusual to be sure, since until that time he had been a secular diplomat. The pope saw what a capable man Contarini was and wanted to bind him to the Holy See in order to lead the pope's reform initiatives. Contarini accepted Pope Paul's offer, but the pope's plan worked better than he hoped. From that point on the new cardinal became more of a papal bureaucrat than the brilliant, independent diplomat he had been. He received the red hat on May 21, 1535, but he had not taken orders. This is not unusual as the rank of cardinal only bestows the right to vote for the next pope in a conclave of cardinals, and does not necessarily require that one be a bishop or even a priest.

The next year, in April 1536, Pope Paul appointed Contarini to lead the commission to study and devise a strategy for reformation. The result of the commission was the document *Consilium de Emendanda Ecclesia,* the Document on the Mending of the Church, which Pope Paul received with great enthusiasm and then circulated among the cardinals, who immediately buried it. Contarini had been encouraged by the pope's attitude, but he and the other Spirituali were naïve about the dynamics of reform. They were seeking reconciliation with the Protestants who by this time weren't interested. They didn't understand that there was more to healing the wounds of Christendom than merely cleaning up abuses within the hierarchy. They actually believed that reform of the papacy and the hierarchy was all that was needed. They did not understand that a new spirit had emerged in the religious West, a spirit that had coagulated into a series of counter-churches, with a completely new understanding of the role of religion in society and in the lives of the people.

In a series of letters to Pope Paul, Contarini complained about the continuing practices of simony and nepotism at the papal court.[6] He complained about continuing schism in the church and of the domination of the church by the papacy. Years later, after the death of Paul III, one of his successors, Gianpietro Carafa, who had been a member of Contarini's reform commission, became Pope Paul IV. Soon after, he instituted the

Index Librorum Prohibitorum, the Index of Forbidden Books, and immediately put the report of that same commission on the list.

Above all, Contarini yearned to restore unity to the church. He
believed that a theological common ground could be found, and he
willingly accepted the evangelical position on justification through
faith. What he could not see was how reform among those in power in
the Catholic Church was being more and more driven by reaction to
the innovations of the Protestants.

In 1541, Contarini was the papal delegate at the Conference of
Regensburg, ostensibly called to try to bring about peace among the
various Christian churches and to hammer out some kind of common
theological statement. The pope sent him with full power to negotiate
peace, but at the same time he harbored a number of hidden reserva-
tions. The emperor was for peace as were the theologians, and so the
members of the conference negotiated a formula that was evangelical
in theology but Catholic in presentation. Everyone at the conference
was pleased by the result and gave their approval.

As this was going on, however, the pope changed his mind about
reunification with the Protestants and informed Contarini of this
change in policy. As the conference broke up, Contarini, in accordance
with the pope's wishes, spoke to the emperor and asked him not to call
another conference without consulting with the pope. To his dismay,
the reactionary movement in the church increased until all attempts
at reconciliation were put aside. Years later, Contarini died in Bologna
while serving as the papal legate, after watching many of his comrades
in the Spirituali flee into Protestant territory to escape pursuit by the
Inquisition. After Contarini died, Ignatius of Loyola acknowledged
that Contarini had been the man behind the approval of the Society
of Jesus, and even after his death, many in Europe praised him for his
mild disposition and his blameless character.

The life of the second great figure in the Spirituali, Bernardino
Ochino, was more tragic. He was born in Siena, and as a boy entered
an order of Observantine Franciscan friars, and with time became the
general of that order. But even there he yearned for stricter discipline
and a tighter rule, so he entered the newly founded Order of Friars

Minor Capuchin. He had already become famous for the fire of his preaching, and for his eloquence of style. As a Capuchin, he joined the circle surrounding Juan de Valdés, who emphasized the mystical life and was drawn to some of the ideas of the Protestant reformers. Ochino quickly became a friend of Vittoria Colonna, the Marchesa de Pescara, and became her spiritual adviser and mentor. He was elected vicar general of the Capuchin order in 1539 and later visited Venice to deliver a series of sermons that strained toward the Protestant position of justification by faith. Later that year, he published a series of dialogues that made it clear that his sympathies were on the side of Protestant theology. Suspicions about his orthodoxy circulated through Rome, and he was denounced there as a heretic. In June 1542, the reactionary Cardinal Carafa instituted the Inquisition in Rome and quickly took action against Ochino.

The Inquisition sent Ochino a letter commanding him to appear before them in Rome, and still considering himself a loyal son of the church he set out in August to obey the summons. Along the way he met with Cardinal Contarini in Bologna, who warned him not to go on to Rome. Contarini was dying, having been poisoned by members of Cardinal Carafa's reactionary party. Following Contarini's advice, he traveled to Florence and from there to the Alps, to Geneva and to Calvin. Calvin received him warmly, and after staying in Geneva for two years, Ochino published a series of tracts defending his change of religion. He also wrote letters to his old friends Vittoria Colonna and Lattanzio Tolomei, who were both sympathizers but who were not willing to follow his path.

The forces of Reformation were beginning to consolidate into opposing sides on the question of justification by faith, which Luther described as the point that decided everything. The politics of Europe would not allow anyone to waffle on this question, and how you decided it determined your direction in Christianity. In 1545, Ochino became a minister for the Italian Protestant congregation in Augsburg, Germany, but in January 1547 the emperor's army occupied that city and Ochino had to flee to England. King Edward VI offered him a position as a prebendary, or senior cathedral priest, in the Cathedral of

Canterbury and bestowed upon him a lifelong pension from the king's privy purse. In England, Ochino composed his *Dialogue of the Unjuste Usurped Primacie of the Bishop of Rome,* which describes a series of debates that take place in hell. Lucifer is furious that Christianity is spreading on earth and calls all the fiends in hell to meet in council, at which they decide to set up the pope as the antichrist. The secular state agrees to assist the pope's assumption of spiritual power, so that the other churches draw away in fear and are intimidated into acquiescence. Suddenly, God sends in his champion, King Henry VIII of England and his son, Edward, to rise up against the antichrist in Rome. This is the beginning of the myth of the pope as antichrist, which has come down to us even today. Milton had most certainly read this work and incorporated some of its ideas into his *Paradise Lost.*

In 1533, Henry VIII's daughter Mary, a Catholic, became Queen of England and attempted to reestablish the Roman church. With the help of Reginald Pole, one of Ochino's old friends in the Spirituali, Mary drove Ochino from England, who then took up residence in Zurich and became a pastor for an Italian congregation living there in exile. Sadly, he increasingly opposed many of the doctrines of the Protestants around him and became disenchanted with Calvinism. He wrote a series of works criticizing the hardening orthodoxy of Protestantism, culminating in the *Labyrinth,* arguing against the Calvinist doctrine of predestination and claiming that the human will was created by God to be free. Ten years later, he published his *Thirty Dialogues,* which incited a storm of opposition. His enemies claimed that he had justified polygamy, and that they found his dialogues on divorce and on the Trinity to be obnoxious. He was banished from Zurich and traveled from one Protestant town to another but was refused asylum. He eventually reached Poland, a nation that was once famous for its tolerance. Then, in August 1564, the king of Poland banished all foreign dissidents, and Ochino fled Poland with his family, who all contracted plague in Moravia. Three of his children died quickly and, finally exhausted by misfortune, he died alone in Moravia in December of 1564. Ochino was at heart a speculative thinker, who worked through theological issues in his dialogues, and although he had been rejected by both the Catholic and the Protestant churches, his passion for free inquiry left a deep impression on the heart and soul of Europe.

Michelangelo had come to adulthood under the influence of Savonarola, and yearned for the reform of the church and the return of the Florentine republic. After the siege of Florence, however, he had abandoned his republican dreams. Vittoria Colonna, a member of the Spirituali, a friend of Ochino, Contarini, and of Reginald Pole, was the one person in the life of Michelangelo who could reawaken him to the reform he had long forgotten.

THOMPSON-NICOLA REGIONAL DISTRICT LIBRARY SYSTEM

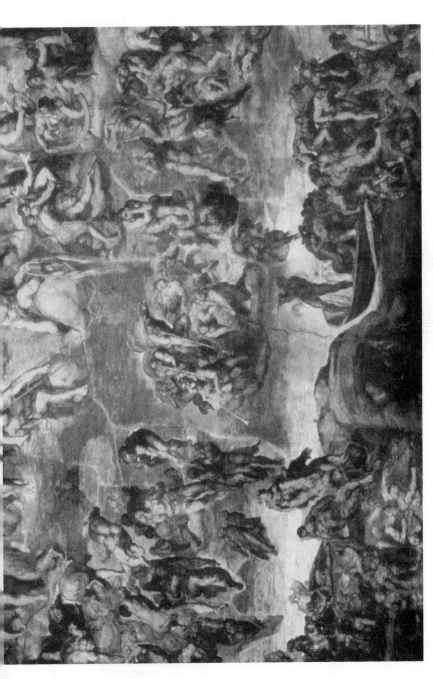

The Last Judgment, with inner and outer orbits surrounding Christ the Judge as the Sol Invictus, the Unconquered Sun. The inner orbit surrounding Jesus is made up of the greater saints, while the outer orbit is made up of the dead, rising from their graves in the left and striving to fly to heaven to join the saved. On the night, the damned fall from heaven toward the underworld. ©Bridgeman Art Library, London / SuperStock

The damned, struggling to remain in the air, but falling toward hell by the weight of to his fate. On the right side: a group of the damned struggle with angels, who keys, indicating his office, and a bag of gold, indicating his avarice. ©Bridgeman Art

heir sins. On the left side: the Reprobate, with one hand covering his face, awakens
ummel them from above. Included in this group is a damned Pope with a set of
ibrary, London / SuperStock

"And I saw the seven angels that stand before God; and there were given to them seven
of days. At the front of the group, two angels hold the books of life and death respectively. Th
their names among the elect, while the book of the damned is shown to the condemne

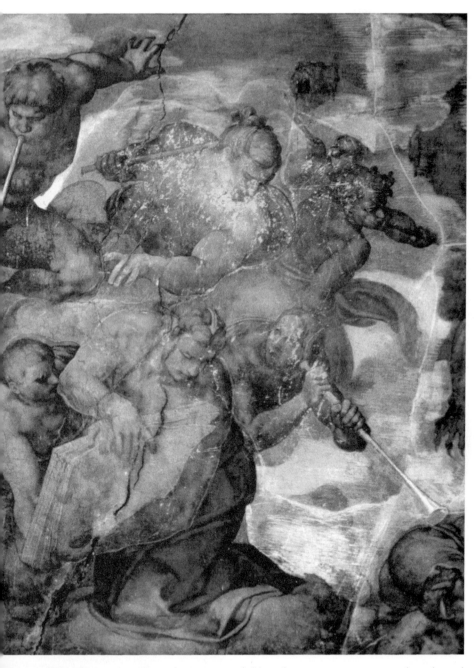

rumpets," Revelations 8:2. Here, the seven angels blow the seven trumpets, signaling the end
much smaller book of life is directed toward those climbing to heaven so that they can read
who are falling toward hell. ©SuperStock, Inc. / SuperStock

Christ rises to curse the damned, his arms rotating, the upper hand cursing, the lower hand pointing to the wound in his side as the wellspring of salvation. Beside him is the Blessed Virgin, hugging his side as if fearing the moment of damnation. Behind him is the aureole of the sun. ©SuperStock, Inc. / SuperStock

CHAPTER SEVEN

Vittoria Colonna

The first six years of Michelangelo's final residence in Rome was one of the richest periods in his life. He had surrounded himself with like-minded people who not only appreciated his art but also looked for the reformation of the church. As a former follower of Savonarola, Michelangelo understood the need for reform, for he had spent his adult life dealing with corrupt priests, lascivious bishops, power-hungry cardinals, and nepotistic popes. Family honor rather than the Gospels had been the driving force of the Italian

Renaissance, as the old Italian aristocratic families waged war upon each other in a perpetual seesaw of power and influence. Any family that could command the papacy could also command the greater share of the rewards. Michelangelo's firsthand knowledge of the affairs of the Medici allowed him to see how far the church had strayed from the path and what was needed for it to come back.

In his art, Michelangelo had explored love, eroticism, warfare, and the elegance of the human body. But he had never strayed too far from the church that he both loved and criticized. Of all the friends that he had made in Rome over the years, none affected him like Vittoria Colonna, the Marchesa di Pescara, whose own spiritual journey and enforced solitude seemed to resonate with Michelangelo's whole life. It is most likely that they met in 1536, though it is not known how they were introduced or in what way they became friends. For all of his struggles with homoerotic feelings, there is no doubt that Michelangelo fell deeply in love with her. She was a beautiful woman, but more than that, she had formidable presence, so that almost everyone who met her later declared that she was the most remarkable person they had ever met.

Vittoria Colonna was a daughter of Fabrizio Colonna of the great Colonna clan, an aristocratic family of warriors and churchmen who often crossed the line into rebellion against the papacy. They could trace their history as far back as 1050, when they took over the feudal estate and castle of La Colonna from which they drew their name. They became the thorn in the side of the papacy for the next 500 years.

Pope Sixtus IV, who had the Sistine Chapel built and was the uncle of Julius II who commissioned Michelangelo's ceiling fresco, tried to use another powerful Roman family, the Orsini, to get control of the rebellious Colonnas. Together, they attacked the Colonna fortress of Palliano but failed to take it. The bravery of its defenders drove his army back, and it is said that Pope Sixtus was so angry about his inability to defeat the Colonnas that he lay in his bed, turned his face to the wall, and died. Later, one of Vittoria's many kinsmen, Cardinal Pompeo Colonna, led a column of horsemen into Rome in support of the army of Emperor Charles V during the sack of Rome, but when he saw what had happened to the Eternal City, the city of his ancestors, he wept. His men wanted to join the fray, but he tried to hold them back and to use them to protect what he could of the city.

Vittoria Colonna was the eldest of six children, the only girl in a family of boys who were seven and eight years younger. She stood out among her siblings, alone even then. She was born in April 1490, fifteen years after Michelangelo, in the castle of Marino on the Lago d'Albano, the family's country place, private and tranquil but close to the city, only 12 miles from Rome. As she grew up, she was surrounded by warriors—her entire family was built for struggle. Her father Fabrizio, the Duke of Palliano, had a great reputation as a soldier, crafty and daring. But like all of the Colonnas, he was a soldier of fortune and would take whatever side paid him the most. He was a mercenary, the most honored profession among the nobility.

In 1494, during the war between the French and the Spanish, the Colonna family changed sides and joined the forces of the King of Naples, Ferdinand I, who was allied with the Spanish emperor. Knowing that he was dealing with a man who sold his military skills to the highest bidder, Ferdinand wanted to cement their relationship beyond the oath of fealty, and he arranged a marriage between Fabrizio's daughter Vittoria and Francesco d'Avalos, the son of the Marchese di Pescara. Though the two children were only four years old, they were officially betrothed. The castle of the d'Avalos family was on the island of Ischia, where Francesco was born in 1489. The d'Avalos family were dedicated to the Renaissance and promoted the reading of the classics, even for the women. Because of the betrothal, Vittoria was raised on the island of Ischia alongside Francesco, which nurtured their friendship as they pursued their studies—Vittoria in letters and Francesco in military arts.

As a young woman, Vittoria was tall, with a pretty face and long blond hair. She and Francesco married in 1509, when she was nineteen years old, with a great celebration and all the pomp and ceremony that both families could afford. As dowry, the Colonnas gave the young Marchese di Pescara a bed in the French fashion with curtains of crimson satin and a cross of diamonds. Francesco's gifts to Vittoria included a cross of diamonds with a chain of gold, worth about 1,000 ducats, and an emerald set in gold, costing about 400 ducats. For the next year, Francesco and Vittoria lived comfortably and happily on Ischia.

But Francesco's greatest desire was to earn renown in battle, and he was always looking for a war to run to. He was not really the model husband that Vittoria believed him to be. He quickly built a reputation for bravery and also for treachery. His shield carried the motto, in good Spartan fashion, "with this or on this." Soon, he was off to fight the French in northern Italy and gained the reputation as a bold and sometimes unscrupulous warrior, and one of the Holy Roman Emperor Charles V's top generals. In 1512, during the Battle of Ravenna, Francesco was fighting at the head of his troops when he was wounded in a number of places, fell off his horse, and lay unconscious on the battlefield. The enemy assumed he was dead, so he lay there for some time, the battle frenzy raging around him, until someone noticed he was alive. Unfortunately, it was a French soldier who carried Pescara off the battlefield as his prisoner.

This was not a good day for Vittoria because her father, who was then the Grand Constable of Naples, had been captured as well and ended up in the same prison as her husband, in the fortress of Porta Gobbia in Milan. When news of this double catastrophe reached Ischia, Vittoria complained in a letter to Pescara set in iambic verse about his absence:

> Oh you men! You think of nothing
> but your honor, and you charge off, shouting
> with blood lust, to confront danger.
> While we remain at home, alone, fearful and
> misery showing on our faces; sister longs for
> brother, wife for husband, mother for son....[1]

Pescara's wounds were serious enough that it took him many months to recover, and during that time he amused himself by writing a long poem, a dialogue on love, and sent it to his wife. No one knows how long Vittoria's husband and father remained in captivity, but eventually through the aid of the Duke of Ferrara, who owed his life to Vittoria's father, Fabrizio, and with the aid of a fortune in ransom, the French set the two heroes free and they rode south toward Ischia. Their return delighted Vittoria. Everyone on the island remarked how Pescara's noble wounds and the paleness of his face made him seem that much more glorious and more desirable. One of the women living on the island, Isabella D'Aragona, told everyone that she wished that she were a man and that she too had a wound like Pescara's so that her face could be as handsome as his.[2] In spite of his warm welcome, Pescara remained on Ischia only for a few months and returned to the war in 1513, along with Fabrizio and Prospero Colonna.

Meanwhile, Vittoria remained on Ischia and continued her studies amidst the orange and olive groves, walking along the Tyrrhenian Sea and atop the cliffs that towered over her island. The couple never had children, which was a constant source of sorrow for her. When Pescara returned from the war, once more the hero, Vittoria was overjoyed to see him. The King of Naples rewarded him by making him the royal chamberlain, and Emperor Charles V piled honors and riches upon him.

Pescara's ambitions, however, soon got the better of him. He became involved in a Milanese plot against the emperor when the conspirators, who claimed they wished to free Italy from the emperor's rule, offered him the crown of Naples. Vittoria was furious with him, for his hubris dishonored her as much as it did him. By November 1525, having failed to convince the nobles of Milan to swear allegiance to Charles V, Pescara was killed during the siege of an important Milanese citadel and died a traitor's death. Vittoria's long period of mourning began.

From this point on, she dedicated herself to poetry and religion, traveling around Italy and staying in various monasteries and convents in Rome, Orvieto, and Viterbo. Her fame as a poet grew, alongside her fame as a great personality and as a reformer of the church.

Vittoria returned to Rome in 1529, and for the next few years she traveled back and forth between Rome, Orvieto, and the island of Ischia. Numerous suitors approached her, but she rejected them all, preferring to live the life of a holy widow and to keep the memory of her dead husband alive. It was at this time that she made friends with some of the greatest leaders in the Catholic Reformation. The group she belonged to, the Spirituali, included Bernardino Ochino, who wanted to open a dialogue with the Protestants, and Reginald Pole, an English cardinal who opposed Henry VIII's schism from Rome and who eventually became a Protestant-hunter under Queen Mary. All of these men and women were educated in the values of the Renaissance and deeply committed to the idea of reforming the church.

The man who affected Vittoria's spiritual thinking more than any other was Juan de Valdés, a priest and noted theologian from Spain who agreed with Luther's idea of justification by faith. This concept was one of the cardinal differences between Catholics and Protestants, because in its early days the Protestant movement, especially the Lutherans, wanted to revive the ancient Christian idea of universal salvation. Throughout the history of Christianity there have been two opposing viewpoints struggling for dominance within the Christian world. The first is the oldest notion that came most directly from the teachings of Jesus and from the church's reflections on his death and resurrection. As St. Paul said in the Letter to the Romans, Christians were freed from the requirements of the Mosaic Law and were justified simply by their faith in Jesus. Later theologians, especially St. Augustine, had to deal with the ongoing problems of the world, and the simple view of justification by faith alone was gradually buried. Part of the reform was to recover this early

Christian ideal—that one had to simply attach oneself to Christ in order to be saved.

Vittoria's contacts with the Spirituali gave her a new direction in life, and she dedicated herself to a life of prayer and contemplation. It was probably contemporaneous with her involvement with this circle of friends, around 1536, that she encountered Michelangelo, the man who painted like God. He had been painting the *Last Judgment* for nearly a year when they met, and there was an instant connection between them. She began to tell him of her rediscovered faith. Michelangelo was immediately taken as much by the force of her personality and the depth of her faith as by her physical beauty, and he fell deeply in love with her. For her part, Vittoria sought to bring Michelangelo into the sphere of the Spirituali, to involve him in the reform in ways that he had never done before. During that period in her life, Vittoria did not stay in one city very long, but traveled from one place to another, often staying in convents where she sought the serenity of the life of a consecrated virgin. For the next few years, she and Michelangelo exchanged letters and, on several occasions, gifts.

A few years later, Michelangelo presented her with two of his drawings. The first was a charcoal sketch of Christ on the cross and the second was a Pièta. In these two sketches he created an aesthetic to fit the new reform spirituality, which was something he was also doing in the *Last Judgment*. Both sketches were made with black chalk and were without color, and yet they were remarkable for their *colorito,* or finish. Michelangelo had drawn the lines of each sketch so finely and with such grace that they suggested the reality of skin. In these two sketches, he took the art of the simple drawing to a new place. Vittoria was thrilled with his gifts and praised the softness of line and the near invisibility of each stroke.

This triggered a conversation between Vittoria and Michelangelo about the relationship between *disegno* and *colore*, or drawing and finish, which was expressed in their correspondence and poetry.[3] This was largely a discussion about the relationship between form and emotion in painting, and both Vittoria and Michelangelo agreed that form should dominate, and that painting should not be a naked appeal to emotion.

This raised a further discussion about the appropriate place between emotion and intellect in the contemplation of Christ's passion, for his two drawings depicted the most emotionally charged scenes in Christian iconography—Christ hanging from the cross, abandoned by his friends, and the scene of his mother mourning over the body of her dead son. Michelangelo depicted the scenes without blood or tears, and yet he expressed their emotion more passionately than had been done by other artists who had employed such easy conventions. Michelangelo had given voice to his own spirituality in the best way he could, and from that point on, everything he created, whether in painting or sculpture or poetry, was a prayer.[4] As he painted the *Last Judgment*, he began to reflect more and more of the early Catholic Reformation ideas into his work.

In 1539, at sixty-four years of age, Michelangelo had left a great deal of his youthful erotic passion behind, and now all of that intense fire was directed toward God. This could be seen in his poetry.

> Freed from a difficult and grave corpse,
> my dear Lord, I turn to you,
> as a weary, broken boat
> set adrift from the world
> sails from the storm toward the sweet calm.[5]

As he later admitted, he owed the revitalization of his spirituality to Vittoria Colonna, who was, above all, a spiritual friend. In the sketches and in his later work, Michelangelo expressed the ambiguity that the Catholic reformers had about realistic depictions of the passion. This was at odds with the growing Spanish tendency to depict the passion in ever more realistic and gory details, full of sweat and blood and open wounds, all designed to invoke pity and a sense of personal responsibility for the sufferings of Christ. The Spirituali, who in our modern terms might be called liberals, agreed with the Lutherans that Christians should be focused on the glorious Christ, as on the day of his resurrection and ascension. In these simple chalk drawings, Michelangelo attempted to create a vision of Christ, even the dead Christ, that was almost radiant rather than grotesque. Though Michelangelo had intended these two sketches to be for Vittoria alone, they were very quickly passed around among the intellectual elite of the Catholic Reformation and became the topic of conversation for some time.

Everything was in flux in those days, especially the idea of reform. As would happen with the Lutherans in Germany, the Catholic Reformation began to divide into two camps, those who wished to hold useful conversations with the growing Protestant movement— indeed, incorporating some of their ideas into Catholic doctrine—and those who wished to redefine the boundaries of Christendom in such a way that it would treat the Protestants as heretics and rebels rather than fellow Christians. Sadly, it was the second movement in the church that began to dominate in the last years of Michelangelo's life.

Vittoria's long-time mentor, Bernardino Ochino, left the Capuchin order and in 1542, after being summoned by the Inquisition, traveled north to join the Protestants. Ochino wrote a letter to Vittoria defending his actions, but she decided that while her own sentiments were in agreement with Ochino's, she would remain loyal to the church. Fearing accusations of heresy might be directed to her, she showed the letter to the local inquisitor. In spite of this precaution, rumblings of heresy concerning her circulated—but she was never formally tried or convicted.

In the late summer of 1539, an amazing set of conversations took place in the church of San Silvestro in the Quirinal district of Rome. The church, located along the Via Quirinal, was dark and cool and had a lovely garden. It was a favorite place for quiet intellectual conversation and was frequented by Vittoria Colonna and others. Michelangelo was a regular at Mass there, because he loved to hear the sermons of Fra Ambroglio, a well known scholar of scripture. After an exhausting week of painting and titanic labor, he often spent his Sundays, his one day of rest, taking a siesta after Mass in the garden of San Silvestro, overlooking the center of Rome. The cloister garden there had a little stream running through it, and he could sit under the trees in his old felt hat and woolen cloak and sleep in the sun.[6]

One Sunday afternoon, Vittoria Colonna met with two men, Lattanzio Tolomei, a humanist and a member of the Spirituali, and Francisco de Hollanda, a young Portuguese painter who had been sent to Rome by the King of Portugal to study the art that graced that city. Francisco would eventually write his recollections of these conversations that often included Michelangelo Buonarroti.[7] While any such record—especially those written several years after the event—may vary somewhat from the true story, we can be sure that they were fairly accurate because de Hollanda candidly portrayed himself as a brash young man, characterized by a combination of hero worship and impetuosity. These recollections are the only record we have of conversations that took place during the period when Michelangelo was painting the *Last Judgment*. As such, they are the clearest windows we have into the artist's mind at that time. His thoughts on art, spirituality, and his own life are laid out there. Since he wrote few letters during this period, these dialogues swell in importance.

They begin with de Hollanda's arrival at the Church of San Silvestre. De Hollanda had been brought there by Tolomei, who wanted to introduce him to Vittoria Colonna, for she had already achieved fame throughout Europe. But Vittoria could see from the first that most of all, de Hollanda wanted to meet Michelangelo. This was particularly difficult because Michelangelo took pains to avoid even his friends. Tolomei admitted to de Hollanda that Michelangelo often kept his distance. Though the two men had been friends for years, Michelangelo found Tolomei's presence too attractive and felt that it made him unable to focus on his art.[8]

Michelangelo had been passing near the church on the Via Esquilina, lost in philosophical conversation with his assistant Urbino, when the Marchesa's messenger approached him, inviting him to join Vittoria Colonna and her company, and he was caught. He couldn't refuse without having a good reason, and so he at least had to make an appearance. Vittoria knew him well enough—once the conversation started, he would warm up to it. Since Michelangelo was reluctant to talk about art especially in front of another artist, he would have to be maneuvered into conversation, which Vittoria Colonna proceeded to do.[9] De Hollanda described how he had whispered into Lattanzio Tolomei's ear that the Marchesa seemed masterful in luring Michelangelo into conversation, how she talked about little things, about events in the city, and the activities in their mutual circle of friends. De Hollanda wrote that it was like watching a general surround and besiege a city, something that he could see Michelangelo was well aware of, as he stood warily waiting for the final assault.[10]

Eventually, the Marchesa praised Michelangelo's generous nature, a characteristic that all his friends knew well. Michelangelo responded that not everyone felt so about him. His complaint was likely in response to a new wave of gossip by some people in the city, largely disgruntled assistants and other lesser painters who wanted his attention, who spread reports of his difficult personality. Michelangelo felt it was necessary to defend his brusque nature.[11] He argued that painters are often strange and unbearable in their manner, though this is a false impression because at heart they are really humane.[12]

Fools, he said, chatter about difficult artists, and consider them to be fantastic creatures, full of caprice and unreasonable whim. But a man who is any kind of painter is a busy man, whose skills are in great demand. Great artists are unsociable not from pride, nor from some deep sense of their own superiority, but from dedication to their art.[13] Michelangelo admitted that there were some practices that required wholehearted devotion, that the practitioner must give himself over to it with such passion that it becomes the master. Painting was one of these he said, and since he was a dedicated painter and a dedicated sculptor he could do nothing else but practice his art. Michelangelo then went on to state that his personality and craft required an avoidance of ceremony and the pretense of the court. If some people saw him as distant, that did not matter.

Vittoria Colonna turned the conversation onto a safe subject, because she knew that Michelangelo's reputation was a sensitive issue for him. She raised the question of Flemish painting, which was safe enough since everyone in the conversation but Francisco de Hollanda was Italian and wouldn't be offended. She went on to say that Flemish painting was excellent in quality, and wondered how it compared to the art of the Italians, which of course, excelled over everyone. Painting done by the Flemish, while technically sound, strove for exactness and wasted its energy on mundane things rather than spiritual things—paintings of cups and of shadows cast by trees and old women standing in the street. While these things were excellent in themselves, and would please some people, they could not be compared with Italian art, since the Italians concerned themselves with the big issues—life and death, salvation and damnation. The Flemish painters, then, appealed to the uninitiated, the hoi polloi, while the Italians, she said, who had the advantage of centuries of culture, reaching back into antiquity, would be naturally more inclined to paint images of greater import than others.[14]

At this point, Vittoria Colonna returned to Flemish painting, saying that it seemed more devout than Italian painting and appealed so readily to the emotions.[15] Flemish paintings would therefore appeal far more to the devout, not through the quality of the painting itself but because of the devout emotions that good people feel when they see them. Flemish works would have strong appeal especially to old women and young women, and largely for the same reasons they would appeal to monks and nuns and to certain kinds of noblemen who have no sense of art. She said no people on earth except for one or two Spaniards have ever attained the level of mastery achieved by Italian painters.

Vittoria Colonna then brought up a subject dear to Michelangelo, that is, the relationship between painting and spirituality. These works gladden the depressed and give life to the lukewarm souls.[16] Such works incite the "melancholy to gladness, and bring knowledge of the human condition to both the contented and troubled alike." At this point, she made reference to Michelangelo's current labor, the subject of much speculation in the city, the *Last Judgment*. Sacred painting "incited conversion in the sinner and inspired the worldly to live for higher concerns."[17] Carrying on her reference to Michelangelo's ongoing fresco, the Marchesa observed that sacred painting revealed our true nature and the inevitability of death, as well as the glory of the blessed and the torments of the damned, laying out both hell and heaven in all of their *terribilità*.[18]

Moreover, she said, alluding to Michelangelo's earlier Sistine Chapel ceiling fresco, that painting allowed us to see God in his glory, to "the modesty of saints, the constancy of martyrs, and the purity of virgins."[19] Painting made even the dead present to us, those whose bones have long decayed, as if they were alive and moving, so that we could note and imitate the great deeds of the past. Painting could set before our eyes the form of any great man, living or dead, allowing us to see depicted on a wall or on canvas those deeds we have heard about.

At this point, the Marchesa had grown melancholy and was close to tears, because her conversation had approached the deep sadness in her life in the death of her husband. But after a few seconds she gathered her emotions and continued to say that painting consoles the widow and allows her to see the portrait of her dead husband, and allows the orphans to see the image of their dead father, to know him as he was. Soon after, the conversation ended and the friends went their separate ways.

Francisco de Hollanda knew that as a young painter he had been privileged to enter into a conversation with Michelangelo, and hoped that the four of them would be able to gather again the next day. Alas, this couldn't happen because Michelangelo had to return to his labor in the Sistine Chapel. So he had to wait until the following Sunday when they gathered again in the quiet chapel of San Silvestro, and resumed the conversation. After they exchanged pleasantries, de Hollanda asked permission to carry on as they had done the week before, inquiring of Michelangelo what he thought were the greatest

works of art in Italy. Michelangelo said that question would take some
time to answer because everyone, from the nobleman to the common
man wanted to possess a little piece of Italian art, and so the best works
were scattered all over Italy.[20] He then talked about works he had seen
in Siena and in Florence, grotesques by Giovanni da Udine and even
some of the finer works by Sebastiano del Piombo, a glorious painting
of the triumph of Julius Caesar in the house of the Duke of Mantua
great works in Venice as well as in Genoa, especially in the house of
Prince Doria.

The Marchesa interjected, pointing out that Michelangelo had
avoided mentioning his own work by skipping Rome entirely.[21] She
was one of the few people who could tease Michelangelo so blatantly
in public. Nothing could be compared to his vault in the Sistine
Chapel, where Michelangelo had depicted how God created the world
and had set forth the long march of salvation starting with Adam,
moving to Noah, and then to the history of the Jews and the coming
of Christ. Moving into more painful territory, because Michelangelo's
last years in Florence had not been a happy time, she pointed out how
he had also omitted mention of his work in the Medici tombs and of
his great sculptures there of *Day* and *Night,* depicted as a man and
woman mournfully ticking off the days, pointing to the inevitability
of death.[22]

Lattanzio, puzzled, said that Michelangelo's sculpture in the
Medici tomb had been described as a part of painting, and wondered
if one could easily conflate the two art forms. This was an idea that
Giorgio Vasari later explored in his book on artistic technique, where
he identified painting with design, something as useful to technology
as to art.[23] De Hollanda was of the opinion, and he believed it to be
Michelangelo's as well, there is really only one art, the art of painting,
because all other art forms begin with painting and depend upon it.[24]
A sculptor must first put his ideas onto paper, drawing models and
sketches of what he intends. An architect relies even more on painting,
for he must draw detailed plans of whatever building he creates. So
that if a great draftsman like Michelangelo carved in marble, and did
so better than he painted with a brush on wood, he would be able to

carve in stone, in hard marble and in bronze and silver, because he is first of all, a draftsman.

Michelangelo supported de Hollanda, saying that a master painter would have to be educated in all of the liberal arts as well as in the sciences relating to architecture and sculpture, and would have to excel in all the other manual arts, even over those who regularly practice them.[25] The art of painting, therefore, was a universal sovereign, queen of all the works of arts and sciences, including writing and history. If human actions were to be considered carefully, he continued, one would soon find that they depended on painting, or were in some form or other an act of painting. The painter would have skills that others would not, and while he could compete with them in their own sphere, they could not compete with him in his.

Lattanzio responded that many people would consider painting to be dumb poetry, unable to speak or to communicate clearly. This was a common jibe leveled at painters, often by poets, who thought that words communicate more precisely than images. At this point, Lattanzio was stepping into deep water, because the group contained two painters, Michelangelo and de Hollanda, and two poets, Michelangelo and Vittoria Colonna. It is possible that the jibe was meant to get a rise out of the young de Hollanda, who would want to defend his art form. It worked. De Hollanda took the bait, saying that such people were wrong and showed that they were simply unskilled in painting. He maintained that poetry was the dumb art, and not painting. Vittoria, untainted by sculpture or painting, rose to defend her own art, asking de Hollanda to lay out his arguments and prove to her that poetry was dumb while painting was not. De Hollanda, making a strategic retreat, demurred, saying he was only a young man with a poor education, and that the Marchesa had asked him to defend the great lady, painting, his one true love, and he felt inadequate to the task, adding that he spoke not as an enemy of poetry because he was deeply indebted to it. However, he argued, not wanting to retreat too far, good poets only say in words what painters actually create, and what the painter creates, the poet can merely express after the fact. Poets, with their lengthy verses, don't always grab the ear, but painters most always give pleasure to the eye by creating a lovely spectacle.

The discussions resumed two weeks later, after a great festival took place in Rome at the Piazza Navona. The occasion was the marriage of Signor Ottavio, the grandson of Pope Paul III, to the Lady Margaret, the adopted daughter of Emperor Charles V. She had been married to Alessandro de Medici, the late Duke of Tuscany, who had been murdered by his cousin, leaving poor Lady Margaret, who was still beautiful, bereft. Everyone said that this was an auspicious marriage, and so the entire city turned out to celebrate, with parties, dances, and banquets throughout the night, with torches and fires burning throughout the city so that Rome seemed to glow in the dark. To demonstrate their greatness, both the emperor and the pope spent lavishly for the wedding. By day, the Pope staged spectacles in St. Peter's Square, and horse races from the Via di Santa Maria di Trastevere all the way to the papal palace. There was a parade of triumphal cars, decked out in gold, with important Roman citizens dressed in ancient fashion, wearing velvet doublets and velvet capes, followed by a hundred sons of the aristocracy on horseback, as if the entire scene were a painting.

After the parade went by, de Hollanda's mind turned toward his recent conversations with Michelangelo and the Marchesa. He sent his servant to San Silvestro to inquire about his friends, hoping that either Michelangelo or the Marchesa would be there. When he arrived, Michelangelo and Lattanzio Tolomei were just coming out of the church, walking toward the garden, so that they could spend the afternoon sitting among the trees and listening to the running water. Both men congratulated Francisco on his wisdom in avoiding the crowds to sit for a quiet afternoon in the garden. Nearby, there was a stone bench beneath some laurel trees covered with ivy, and enough room for the three of them to sit comfortably and look out over the city caught in the midst of celebrating.

The Marchesa's messenger, a young man named Signor Zapata, begged them to continue with the conversation they had started two weeks before,[26] because even though the absent Marchesa did not wish to intrude, she had sent Zapata to the garden to do just that. Certainly,

Zapata would return to the Marchesa and tell her everything that everyone said. De Hollanda responded that Michelangelo was under no obligation to respond to the wishes of the Marchesa, because in a previous conversation she had said that the art of painting was useless during wartime, a comment he strongly disagreed with and he had expected her to come to explain her words.[27]

Michelangelo told de Hollanda that nothing could be more important to the art of war than the art of painting. After all, it was a painter, namely himself, who had designed the defenses of Florence when Pope Clement and the emperor besieged that city,[28] and because of his designs the ultimate fall of the city was postponed for months, perhaps even years. After all, the art of painting is used in designing the machines of war—catapults and battering rams and tortoises and towers, as well as in the fashioning of cannons and harquebusiers. All of the machinery of war begins in painting, from the design of armor to the painting of heraldry on shields. Michelangelo then appealed to Alexander the Great who consulted the genius of the Greek painter Apelles in helping him draw the plans for his campaign.

Zapata then asked Michelangelo to speak about the usefulness of painting in peace.[29] Michelangelo said that during peacetime idle princes liked to divert themselves with foolish things and to surround themselves with people of no real talent except the talent to make profit on other people's misfortunes. In independent states and republics, he observed, the Senate often employed painting for public needs, to decorate the cathedrals, the courts of justice, the porticos and basilicas, even the palaces of the wealthy. The wealthy often employed artists to decorate their country homes as well, to display their artistic taste and refinement. In such states, no one is allowed to gather enough power to exalt himself over the others, and painters are given commissions that make them wealthy. Even in good-hearted and peaceful kingdoms, God has given power to one individual to build lavish works for the public good and for their own honor, for a prince would subvert his own power if he did not give such works to his kingdom during peacetime.[30] Michelangelo cited as an example Augustus Caesar, who spent more gold during peacetime than during wartime as he adorned the Palatine Hill and the Forum with great and wonderful works of architecture and art.

De Hollanda then observed that he had heard that Augustus Caesar had paid for one set of painted figures the same amount of money that he had paid for a company of soldiers.[31] In Spain, he said, they would find it more difficult to believe anyone would pay that kind of money for art than to believe that in Italy there are painters who are so awful that they would paint the emperor with the legs of a crab. Michelangelo laughed and said that he knew that in Spain they paid less for art than they did in Italy, and that this was why there were more painters in Italy than in Spain. The Spaniards, he said, are the strangest people: Their nobility went into ecstasies about painting and the arts, but they protest that they have no money for such things. Michelangelo advised de Hollanda, that if he wished to pursue the art of painting, he needed to live in Italy and not return to Spain or Portugal—that every painter should wish to live in Italy and no place else.

Vittoria Colonna would live another eight years, until February 25, 1547. The last five years of her life she lived in fear of the Inquisition, for though she decided to remain a loyal Catholic, her friendship with Bernardino Ochino would cast a shadow of suspicion over her, and she hid her strongly held beliefs that many Lutheran ideas were holy and valuable for the Christian soul. Michelangelo outlived her by two decades, and after she died, he grieved her loss for the rest of his life. The one thing he regretted was that on her deathbed he did not kiss her goodbye.[32]

CHAPTER EIGHT

Sol Invictus

For Michelangelo, the Sunday conversations in the quiet church of San Silvestro were only an interlude, a relaxing break from his work. Even while laughing or discoursing on art with Vittoria Colonna and Francisco de Hollanda or passionately defending his way of life to all present, Michelangelo's mind never left the great work on the altar wall of the Sistine Chapel. Six days a week he walked out of his house while it was still dark, accompanied only by his faithful servant and student Urbino, trudged around the capital, across the Ponte

Sant'Angelo, past the statues of Peter and Paul erected by Pope Clement, through the piazza in front of St. Peter's, which was still under construction, to the Sistine Chapel, where he would lock himself and his assistant inside, opening the door only for the pope. Climbing the scaffolding, he would paint through the day and long into the night, barely stopping for meals, while Urbino ground and prepared the colors for his master.

Money for the scaffolding was paid in April 1536, after nearly a year's delay because of the difficulties with Sebastiano del Piombo. The documents record this, showing that Sebastiano's *intonaco* was destroyed on January 25, 1536. On February 13, the Vatican then paid a kilnman, Gioanni Fachino, to supply bricks for Michelangelo's rebuilding of the wall.[1] The scaffolding was erected fairly quickly because the structure was not nearly as complicated as it had been when he painted the Sistine Chapel—where the scaffolding had to be mounted and dismounted and mounted again as he worked his way across the ceiling. This time, the scaffolding only had to be erected bit by bit and then disassembled bit by bit as Michelangelo worked his way from the lunettes near the ceiling to the ground.

While the new wall preparation was being completed, Michelangelo sent in his first order for pigments, on May 18, 1536. The order of painting Michelangelo used was boustrophedon, an ancient style that imitated the motion of an ox plowing a field first from left to right and then back again. This was the pattern of early Greek writing, so that the eye never left the page, scanning back and forth.

The first figures Michelangelo painted were of the obscure heads of four angels in the upper left lunette, peeking over a pair of figures near another group of angels who are carrying the cross to the scene of judgment, and from there to the other lunette with angels carrying the pillar of Christ's scourging. Altogether, there are 456 *giornate* in the fresco. One *giornata* is the section of wall that can be painted in one day. The fact that the *giornate* appear to flow together suggests that he worked steadily, without many pauses. Michelangelo painted the lunettes and then paused, which is visible in the difference between the levels in the surface. Also, Michelangelo took time to complete the cartoon for the central figure of Christ.[2]

Dramatically, the center of the fresco is the titanic figure of Christ, the Son of God, in the form of Apollo, the sun god, and the universe, heaven and hell, earth and sky, struggling to receive him. The person of Christ is the fulcrum of the painting, setting all things moving. In Aristotelian language, he is the unmoved mover, the one who begins all the action, the one around whom all the action swirls. The arrival of the Son of God is the catalyst, initiating the drama, setting the universe spinning, commencing the catastrophe, and all those who surround him stare at him in awe and in terror. He is perfect action and inaction set in balance, ambiguously half-sitting, as if he is rising from a throne. Instead of being clothed with lordly robes, Jesus enters the world naked, except for a single cloth draped across his loins.[3]

The nakedness of Michelangelo's Christ is directly inspired by the ancient Greek texts and sculptures. For the Greeks, the gods were perfect, and the best way to depict that perfection was to sculpt them or paint them naked. Their nakedness was a sign of their perfection because the gods had nothing to hide. Young Greek men who attended the gymnasium exercised in the nude to show off the perfection of their bodies, mere mortals aspiring to look like the gods. Public nakedness was not a problem for the Greeks if it was done in the appropriate place. The gymnasium, the baths, sometimes even in combat—the young Greek men displayed all without shame or confusion.

Thousands of years later, the Italian Renaissance tried to resurrect Greek culture and to rediscover Greek and Roman ideals. While public nakedness was still frowned upon, depicting it in art demonstrated the artist's bona fides as a Renaissance humanist. One of Michelangelo's direct influences when he was painting the *Last Judgment* was the series of frescos on the same subject painted between 1499 and 1503 by Luca Signorelli in the Cathedral at Orvieto. Signorelli painted a large number of nude figures in his frescos, which stand as transitions between the static Byzantine and Medieval apocalypses and Michelangelo's highly dynamic, dramatic fresco on the altar wall of the Sistine Chapel. While these frescos were striking in their time, the nude figures raised few concerns.

Moreover, three decades earlier, no one had complained about Michelangelo's *David*. This was because he was patterned after the Greek ideal of perfection—a young man in the glory of his youth and vitality, displaying the perfection of his body. But Michelangelo's *Last Judgment* was painted thirty years later, as all of Europe was readying itself to wash away all of the old corruption in the waters of reform. This made his startling new fresco a transitional work and, to the growing consciousness of the counterreformation, a dangerous one. At the heart of the Reformations, both Protestant and Catholic, was a growing sense of the centrality of the Scriptures, and there were no Greek philosophers in the Bible. Therefore, the counterreformation sensibility about nudity was far more biblical than Greek, and such a blatantly Renaissance depiction of the Son of God by the foremost painter in Europe in the papal chapel itself was bound to turn heads.

Michelangelo had good theological reasons to paint the majority of his figures in the nude, for he was not trying to depict bodies as much as souls. The Greeks used the perfect human form to depict the gods, Michelangelo used the human body to depict the human soul. This is why Michelangelo's artworks so rarely made raw appeals to emotion and were never sentimental, but always titanic. The final purpose of art is always to depict that which cannot be understood any other way. The poet uses metaphor; the artist uses symbols; the musician gathers exquisite arrangements of sound. The human soul is invisible and can only be made visible by the painter's brush.

Spirituality was never a matter of sentimentality for Michelangelo. His own spirituality was overflowing with *terribilità,* power and glory, like the sun rising in the morning or like a thunderstorm building on the horizon. In nearly all of Michelangelo's works, he reached for the sublime through the mystery that terrifies and fascinates. Jesus was rarely the Good Shepherd coming in from the fields, full of serenity and joy. Jesus, like his companions in art, was twisted and torn in the dramatic tension that depicted human life as a war. The Jesus of the *Last Judgment* was not a nice Jesus or a pleasant Jesus, but one coming upon the clouds of heaven, the Son of God at the end of the world, terrible as an army set in battle array. His face is dispassionate, almost blank, as if the condemnation of evil and the consignment of thousands of souls to eternal fire did not affect him. His *terribilità* had taken him above the common joys and fears of the human race, for in that moment he was revealed as God, terrible in his mystery, fearful in his power.

Like everyone else in Michelangelo's art, Christ is bulging with muscles. This particular fresco of Michelangelo's is noteworthy for the exaggerated musculature of all of his figures. Even the women seem to be loaded with muscles and near masculine in their strength. Part of this may have to do with Michelangelo's technique, which he used both in the *Last Judgment* and in his ceiling fresco. When he had finished a figure, most commonly a nude, Michelangelo would inevitably return to it to amplify the form, as if his nudes were never big enough. Sometimes, these expansions would increase the size of the body part by a number of centimeters. But once again, Michelangelo had theological reasons for depicting his figures in this way, reasons that had more to do with the nature of the soul than of the body. As he rises into action, Jesus' face is turned toward the damned, as if he is caught in the middle of condemnation. His left hand points toward the blessed, while his right hand, is raised above his head, palm open. As if with a gesture of denial, he is waving the doomed away from him.

Next to him is his mother, seated at his side, no longer kneeling before him to intercede on behalf of the poor souls in purgatory, but leaning toward him, trying to get as close as possible. Both of them seem to be standing on clouds turning into stone, as if wherever the divine judge steps he is solid on his feet. Mary's hands are crossed before her face in a medieval attitude of prayer. Her face is turned away from the damned, as if she cannot bear to watch their condemnation. She is, as she has always been in Christian iconography, the last refuge of sinners, the defenders of those who, with sincere hearts, have not achieved the holiness needed for salvation. In other words, she is the defender of all of us. But here, at the end of all things, her task as the refuge of sinners is over and she clings to her divine son as if she were part of him.

In some ways, these two figures seem to stand alone, but they are also surrounded by a group of saints—John the Baptist, Saint Peter,

Saint Paul, Saint Lawrence, and Saint Bartholomew. There are 103 *giornate* making up this group, not counting corrections and over-painting done *a secco*. Michelangelo, or possibly Urbino, transferred the cartoons to the wall through pouncing—taking a stick and tracing out the lines of the cartoon—applying black powder with a series of dabbing motions, so that outlines of figures appear on the wall as a set of dots. After this, Michelangelo would paint a black line through the dots to create a unified line.

Most of this central group is painted in *buon' fresco,* but there are many corrections, sometimes to deepen a shadow or to change the position of a figure. Most of these corrections—such as the gridiron held by Saint Lawrence, and the blade of the knife held by Saint Bartholomew—are painted *a secco.* Michelangelo also painted over the aureole of light surrounding Christ, the divine judge. The stigmata—the wounds on his hands and feet and the lance wound in his side—were all painted *a secco.* And there is evidence that Michelangelo repositioned the condemning right hand of Christ numerous times, eventually adding heft to the muscles.

Vasari explains that Michelangelo was attempting to paint a fresco that carried the art of the posed nude as far as it could go.[4] But Michelangelo also had theological reasons for painting his nudes in this way. Since the body was a symbol of the soul for Michelangelo, the bulging muscles were indicative of the power of the spirit. Picturing the resurrected people with titanic muscles, therefore, said more about what Michelangelo believed about the human soul than about the human body.

One of the most curious images in this group of figures is the sagging flayed skin of Saint Bartholomew, which many scholars believe depicts Michelangelo's own features. Interestingly, the face of Saint Bartholomew is similar to the face of Pietro Aretino, one of Michelangelo's chief persecutors. The empty skin was painted in one *giornata,* as a single piece, and was repainted *a secco* afterward. In most of these figures, Michelangelo used strong brushstrokes to outline the bodies. However, in this group, for the sake of perspective, Michelangelo varied the size and style of his strokes.[5] Another noteworthy section is the face of the Virgin, for which Michelangelo juxtaposed colors with white lime to create a mottled effect that pre-dated pointillism by hundreds of years. Careless cleaning efforts over the centuries have softened this effect in some places, most notably on the blue mantle of the Virgin, where Michelangelo had used a *secco* technique to deepen the shadows with dark azurite in order to heighten the chiaroscuro effects of the drapery.[6]

In medieval and Renaissance painting it was common enough to depict holy people with halos or aureoles of light surrounding their heads. Michelangelo rejected such easy techniques and sought to depict holiness and strength of soul through facial characteristics and the stance of the body. Except Jesus and the Virgin, no one else in the *Last Judgment* has a halo. The lozenge of light here serves two pur-poses—first, to memorialize the position of the sun in the Copernican universe. The sun for Copernicus was unmoving, and all the planets, including the earth, revolved around it. Here, the figure of Christ is the sun, and all the souls, both blessed and damned, revolve around him.[7] The second purpose is to emphasize Jesus as the sun god. This is why he painted him clean-shaven, as a young man in the prime of his strength. In good Renaissance fashion, Michelangelo depicted the judging Christ as a young Apollo, curly hair and all. This particular choice would cause him no end of trouble in the coming years, because reactionary elements of the Catholic Reformation would object to so radical a departure from tradition.

Until Constantine's time, when Roman soldiers marched lockstep into battle, they carried upon their shields the symbol of Sol Invictus, the Unconquered Sun, lordly and commanding, the ultimate symbol of power. The same symbol quickly became the central axis of the early church's thinking about Christ. In a Christmas troparion (short hymn) the Greek Orthodox Church proclaims Jesus to be the Sun of Righteousness:

> Your birth of Jesus Christ our God
> Has brought the light of truth to the earth
> Because of your nativity those who once worshipped the stars

Were taught by a star to adore the Sun of Righteousness
And to come to know you, the heavenly sunrise
Glory to you, now and forever.[8]

Throughout the Middle Ages, whenever the church wanted to depict Christ in his glory, they show him coming upon the clouds of heaven, transfigured, and shining like the sun. Apocalyptic in its origin, Christianity has long held to the division of the world into the Children of Light and the Children of Darkness, a division that started with the Essenes at Qumran, a radical Jewish sect that separated itself from the shifty politics of Jerusalem to await the coming of the Messiah. It was a sect that, many believe, John the Baptist had joined before taking up residence along the Jordan River. Christian symbolism has thus always connected Christ with light and Satan with darkness.

Accordingly, in Michelangelo's *Last Judgment,* the sun is the center of the universe, and Christ, emerges from the sun as the light to the world, commencing the *Dies Irae,* the Day of Wrath by his presence. This hymn was sung on Good Friday, at every funeral mass, and on the All Souls' Day. It would have been as familiar to Michelangelo as "Amazing Grace" is to us.

One of the earliest concepts of the Last Judgment emerges directly out of Saint Paul's First Letter to the Corinthians, in which all the dead would rise and be given new spiritual bodies. No one really knows exactly what St. Paul meant by that, or knows exactly what a spiritual body would look like, but in Michelangelo's conception, the dynamic power of a spiritual body, especially in the way it transcended the limitations of earthly flesh could only be depicted by exaggerating musculature and setting each figure into a dramatic pose. This is why so many of Michelangelo's figures stand contrapposto, where the torso and the feet seem to be moving in opposite directions.

Michelangelo's figure of Christ is particularly ambiguous in its position. Jesus seems caught between sitting and striding, his right arm and left arm seemed to be moving in opposite directions, as if welcoming the just and condemning the damned. In fact, his arms

seem to pinwheel, resembling a swastika, which for us darkly represents the Nazis and all of their evil deeds, but for Michelangelo and his
contemporaries, living hundreds of years before Adolf Hitler, the swastika was an ancient, even prehistoric, symbol of the sun, a dynamic
symbol that depicts the sun as a dynamic thing, not only shining, but
also rotating.

The face of Jesus is particularly terrifying in its ambiguity, for
when the average Catholic imagines confronting God on the last
day, they certainly want to see a smiling face. Even if God were obviously angry, that would be preferable to the unreadable ambiguity of
Michelangelo's conquering Jesus. It seems impossible to determine his
feelings, whether he is furious or uncaring, detached, as he casts count-
less souls into the eternal fire. His function in the fresco, therefore, is
to be the dynamic center of gravity for all the figures in the scene. The
ambiguity of the judging Christ evokes anxiety in all the characters of
the fresco, even the saints—all are reacting to him, measuring their
lives by him, so that even the best of them suffer from insecurity, like
Michelangelo himself.

CHAPTER NINE

Saints, Martyrs, and Angels

*C*atholic tradition makes a distinction between saints and martyrs. Saints are anyone who makes it to heaven[1]—you can get there by living an exemplary life, dying an exemplary death, living a life of contemplation, living a life of service, or, like Constantine, you can convert on your deathbed. The tradition assumes that there is a great ocean of grace that falls upon the world like rain. This grace is necessary for ordinary people, who make up 99 percent of the human population, who have not lived exemplary lives nor suffered in some extraordinary way, nor gone to some far-off place to assist the poor and downtrodden who live there. Ordinary people live ordinary lives. Nevertheless, the tradition holds that any ordinary person, through the grace of God and some modicum of labor on his or her own part, can attain the glories of heaven. All these people are saints even though they are not canonized. These are the ones we celebrate on All Saints' Day.

Martyrs, on the other hand, are a completely different breed. The word means "to give witness" and to do so dramatically. It also usually means dying violently, in some horrible way. Perpetua and Felicity were both fed to the lions. Saint Peter was crucified upside down. Saint Stephen was stoned to death. There are very few popes who are martyrs, except in the earliest centuries of Christian history, but quite a few who are saints. There are bishops who are martyrs, priests who are martyrs, nuns and even laypeople who are martyrs.

The group surrounding the Son of Man come in glory in Michelangelo's *Last Judgment* fresco is populated largely by martyrs, who also happen to be saints. This is the inner orbit around Jesus, the heroes of the faith. On the left side of the fresco is Saint John the Baptist, balanced by Saint Peter on the right. Unlike the older tradition, John the Baptist is not standing to intercede for the sinners but is looking intently at Christ the judge. On the other side Peter who holds out the keys of the kingdom given to him by Jesus on earth also gazes intently toward Christ. Michelangelo used the face of Pope Paul III to model the face of Peter, which makes political sense, visually connecting the line of the popes from Peter to the reigning Pope Paul. The Papacy has its roots in the tradition of Peter's primacy among the apostles. According to this tradition, Peter was the chief of the apostles, a position given to him by Jesus. When Jesus asked his disciples who they thought he was, Peter answered that he was the Christ, the Messiah, and Jesus said to him, "You are rock and upon this rock I will build my church, and the jaws of death shall not prevail against it. I will entrust to you the keys of the kingdom of heaven. Whatever you declare bound on earth shall be bound in heaven; whatever you declare loosed on earth shall be loosed in heaven."[2] The papacy is the line of Peter's successors, and by the tradition they derive their spiritual authority from him.

On the other side of Christ, standing behind John the Baptist is the figure of Adam, who puts one hand on the arm of the Baptist and peers around him as if hoping to be shielded by him. Tradition holds that the line of those righteous souls who waited for the coming of Jesus began with Adam and ended with the Baptist. On the other side of John the Baptist is the figure of Saint Andrew, with his back to the viewer, carrying his X-shaped cross.

What is remarkable about this fresco is that nearly every face has a unique recognizable expression. Some figures are running toward Jesus and encouraging others to follow; others are turning away in fear. There is one common emotion however. Agitation is on every face—no one is marching serenely into heaven. Rather, it is as if a great cacophony had exploded around the figure of Christ, and everyone is shouting and talking at the same time.

The saints and martyrs around Jesus hold out the instruments of their death—Saint Lawrence carries the gridiron upon which he was roasted alive. Saint Sebastian, in a kneeling position, holds out the arrows that pierced his body. Saint Bartholomew holds a knife in one hand and his flayed skin in the other. Many of them, with the notable exception of St. Sebastian, are turned toward the figure of Christ, and instead of interceding, they are asking for justice. They hold out their instruments of torture as a reminder of what they had suffered, and they call upon Jesus to judge the reprobates, the idolaters, the sinners strictly, to make them suffer in their turn.

To the casual observer, this seems harsh. One would expect that the people who are in heaven, the close intimates of the God who is love, at least according to the first epistle of Saint John, would have more sympathy for poor sinners who did not have the courage to do what they did or to suffer what they suffered.

In depicting the martyrs holding out symbols of their death, calling for salvation, Michelangelo is firmly coming down on the side of justice, perhaps even divine retribution, for the martyrs in this instance are demanding recompense. But is this Christian? The heart of Christianity is that love transcends justice and that God's mercy is greater than ours. This has been the position of the liberal wing of Christianity for centuries, from Justin Martyr to Daniel Berrigan. It was likely the position of the Spirituali, but not of the reactionary wing of the Catholic Reformation. In depicting the martyrs this way, Michelangelo shows himself, unexpectedly, to sympathize with those who would close off all contacts with the Protestants rather than with those who would start an open-hearted dialogue.

This theological choice in his fresco is one of his most radical departures from tradition and says as much about Michelangelo's spirituality as it does about Catholic doctrine. All the figures are moving, twisted and straining into heroic poses, so that in Michelangelo's view the end of the world is not a stately affair, but a time of tears and exultation. This view is not necessarily in line with modern Christian thinking, but it was normal for Roman Christians after the sack of Rome. The sufferings of the citizens naturally cried out for vengeance, vengeance that they would wrap in the mantle of justice.

Michelangelo, however, as was depicted in the fresco, was deeply aware of the variations found in the human response to God. Some of those in the inner circle are fixed upon the person of Christ and are staring at him with fierce attention. Others, including a few in the inner circle, are torn between the presence of Christ and some other concern. To the left of Jesus, near John the Baptist, Saint Andrew is turned away from the viewer and from Christ as he reaches out to a woman dressed in green and white, urging her forward. But the woman is looking over her shoulder as if waiting for someone to arrive, one finger raised as if to say "just a moment." Just behind her, in shadow, is the face of a dark-skinned man, his hands clasped in prayer.

Each one of these characters exhibits a personal response to Christ, which is the heart of the meaning of the fresco. The Christian (and Jewish) traditions hold that there are two great commandments that sum up the whole law and the prophets: "you shall love the Lord your God with your whole heart, with your whole soul, with your whole mind, and the second is: you shall love your neighbor as yourself."[3]

In Michelangelo's depiction of the Last Judgment, some of the Elect are focused passionately on Christ, while some are focused on other people, but all of these responses are essentially the same, since their attention is on love. While those who are watching Christ represent those who have followed the first commandment, and in sixteenth century terms, have lived a contemplative life, those who are turned to help another soul represent those who have followed the second commandment, and have lived an active life. There is another Catholic tradition that holds that even in heaven among the blessed there is a hierarchy of holiness. There are some whose humility is greater and whose love of God is deeper than those who managed to get there after a bout of purgatory. Thomas Aquinas, who greatly admired Aristotle and was therefore fond of hierarchies, mentions this, but the imaginative dimension of the tradition is part of the folklore of Catholicism and does not enter into the doctrine.

What is in the tradition, however, is the notion that the presence of God is overwhelming even for those in heaven who can stand in the divine presence and not be burned by it. All the faces in the inner circle except the face of the Virgin and of the woman dressed in green seem surprised at the presence of Christ. Saint Paul, who stands behind Saint Peter and is wrapped in a red cloth of martyrdom, seems to pull back in astonishment, as if the sudden presence of Christ revealed in glory is more than he ever expected.

Sprinkled among the famous figures is a collection of anonymous persons, some praying, some leaning toward Jesus, some with a hand raised is if they wish to ask a question. Even the elect in the inner circle are filled with agitation as they ask, "What about me, Lord?" They do not seem quite certain that they are part of the elect. Just behind Saint Bartholomew and his Michelangelo-face skin is the figure of a man with gray hair in a saffron cloak.

One theory is that it is the face of Michelangelo's beloved student and servant Urbino.[4] Interestingly, Michelangelo seems to have no questions about his assistant's place on the Day of Judgment. On the other side, almost buried behind the figure of John the Baptist, out of the red drapery at John's feet in the space between John and Andrew pops the face of a white-bearded man. He is looking off to the side, out of the inner circle, with an expression of fear and worry. Perhaps he looking back at the elect in the outer circle struggling to rise from the earth to join with Jesus in the air, or perhaps he feels that he himself might fall backward, might sink from the presence of God, the weight of his own flesh too heavy for him.

We see in such background figures the shape of uncertainty, sometimes out of place. One would expect that anyone who found himself in the inner circle surrounding Jesus would have little to fear, but that is not the truth to be found in the *Last Judgment*. Seeing these haunted faces, alive with anxiety, it is easy to have a moment of fellow feeling with the long dead Michelangelo, who was so adept at giving us a window into his own inner struggle. The fact that Michelangelo had painted his own likeness into the empty skin of Saint Bartholomew, held by the hand of the figure whose face was that of Pietro Aretino, reveals something of his inner life.[5]

Even as Michelangelo painted the *Last Judgment,* he recognized the danger that Aretino, the scourge of princes, the satirist who terrified kings and popes alike, represented. In the fresco, he has Aretino holding out the flayed skin with Michelangelo's face on it, as if Michelangelo expected to be flayed by this difficult man. The skin hangs down in long droopy folds. The hands and feet are extended as if the weight of them has stretched the skin. The face is recognizable as Michelangelo's from the swirls of black hair and the obviously broken nose. Nowhere in the painting of all this vast fresco do we find another self-portrait. Not among the elect, and not even among the damned, only in this bare skin of a saint, who turns toward Jesus and holds up the knife that had cut his skin from his body. The saint's expression is fierce, almost demanding recompense for his suffering. And yet, behind him is a figure of another sort. A naked man turns toward a woman behind him whose head is wrapped in cloth, her face nearly hidden, her hands raised as if to ward off the brightness of the sun. The man in front turns and reaches out—is it to take the shawl from her face?—his other hand held out, cupped in supplication, as if he is quietly insisting that she look upon the face of God.

Here the complexity of Michelangelo's imagined response to Christ is underlined—on one hand he depicts a man looking away from Christ in fear, but at the same time he shows another man urging a woman to look upon Christ, to confront her fear and bask in the moment.

There is a theological idea that has haunted Christianity since its beginning. It is a Greek idea, imported from Iran that has its roots in the old Gnostic sects, whose writings were found in the Nag Hammadi library in Egypt and in some of the Dead Sea Scrolls. The idea sets the spirit and the flesh in opposition, so that the spirit, which is closer to God and, the Gnostics believed, carried a divine spark, needed to be freed from the burdens of the flesh. The flesh is subject to sickness and death, lives in time, and must suffer decay. The spirit, however, is immortal, and the only way to free it is through a renunciation of the body.

When the Greek world encountered this theological idea, the idea became entangled with an already existing Greek physics, originally codified by pre-Socratic philosophers who divided the world into light and heavy. Aristotle took this idea and argued that light things naturally rise and heavy things naturally fall. If you drop a stone into a stream, it will sink to the bottom. If you light a fire, the smoke will naturally rise. Therefore, the sky is the natural place for light things, and the earth is the natural place for heavy things. Light things are made up of fire and air, whereas heavy things are made up of earth and water.

By the time these two ideas filtered down to the Renaissance, they had produced the belief that the soul is something light, while the body is something heavy. Medieval theologians used Saint Paul to support their interpretation, for he said it was the flesh that separates us from Christ and the spirit that brings us closer. "What a wretched man I am," Saint Paul said in Romans 7. "Who will save me from this body doomed to die? Thanks be to Jesus Christ, our Lord and God, who frees us from this world." It is good spiritual discipline, according to this interpretation, to spend your life mortifying the flesh, punishing it for its heaviness and for its constant demands. Sexuality then is seen as lust, hunger becomes gluttony, the desire for comfort becomes avarice. This notion of spirituality is not necessarily wrong, for it has survived for two thousand years and many generations have found it sensible.

Michelangelo suffered greatly from this idea of the spirit and flesh at odds with one another. As he aged, he saw himself as one doomed to suffer the second death of hell with the slight possibility of forgiveness in the end. And yet the biblical passage that the *Last Judgment* is depicting is one where the Son of God judges based on one criterion, and that is the amount of love each person has shown to the poor. The Seven Deadly Sins that so informed the middle ages—Pride, Lust, Avarice, Sloth, Gluttony, Wrath, and Envy—are only obliquely related to the criterion in Matthew 25.[6] "And the wicked shall say to him 'Lord, when did we see you hungry or thirsty or naked or sick or imprisoned or away from home?' and the King will say to them 'As long as you refused to do this to one of my least brothers and sisters, you refused to do it to me.' " He desired holiness, and in desiring it, he began to view his own body as an oppressor.

In this view, it was the flesh that made humanity insane with love, the flesh that filled human life with a panoply of demands. It is the flesh and the sin it carries that twist us, set us off balance like his figures *contrapposto*. Regrettably, this idea has pushed aside the other Christian position that the sins of the flesh are as nothing compared to the sins of the spirit. Although Michelangelo imagined that the elect were people who had sufficiently escaped the wiles of the flesh, Jesus who taught that it is the spirit, the intention of the heart that is the source of both good and evil in human life.

To the right of the inner circle is a group of the elect, gathered in various poses. The largest figure in the foreground depicts Saint Simon of Cyrene, the man who carried the cross for Jesus, with his back to a huge cross, as if he is ready to carry it once again. At his foot and slightly to the left of Saint Sebastian and his arrows are two figures that caused a tremendous amount of controversy. The figures represent Saint

Catherine of Alexandria and Saint Blaise with the instruments of their deaths. Catherine is leaning over a piece of a spiked wheel while Blaise, who stands behind her, carries two wool combs with long tines.

Originally, Michelangelo had painted both figures in the nude, but when the painting was first revealed in 1541, many people complained that the two saints looked as if they were preparing for sex, as if Blaise was saying to Catherine "hold still," and as if Catherine, looking back at Blaise, was replying "What are you doing?" Whether Michelangelo intended this or not cannot be determined for he was quite capable of bawdy humor, having interjected quite a bit of it in his famous ceiling fresco. On the other hand, such an image might be over the top even for him, and the people who complained about the image may have been revealing more about themselves and their own sexual fantasies than they intended. It is easy enough to see sexual images in such a vast sea of naked people. And although he had *ignudi* (naked male figures) as accent points in the ceiling vault fresco, the majority of his figures there are clothed or depicted naked for good theological reason. In the panel of the creation of Adam, for example, both God and Adam are naked, which makes sense because Adam is in a state of innocence before the fall and does not realize that he is naked, while God in his perfection is depicted in the Greek style, with a perfect body that indicates a perfection of spirit. In the *Last Judgment*, however, nearly everyone is naked or semi-naked.

The presentation of naked figures has more to do with Michelangelo's own spirituality than with the Christian tradition of the resurrection of the body—in which the body is the vessel of the soul. The doctrine of the resurrection of the body teaches that at the end of time, each man and woman will rise from the dead and return to a perfected form of their original body, one that cannot die or suffer disease. This would be true even of the damned.

As for the saints, Catherine of Alexandria and Blaise, there may have been a sizable portion of willful misinterpretation. Notwithstanding Michelangelo's penchant for bawdy humor, the idea that he would depict two famous saints about to have sex on the last day seems a bit far-fetched. This particular misreading of Michelangelo's figures created quite a stir, and Michelangelo was accused of painting an obscenity in the pope's own chapel.

Not everything in the fresco is darkness, agitation, and fear, however, for just above the figures of saints Blaise and Catherine is a group of figures who are turning to greet one another. In the front, there are two men, naked except for a small bit of drapery, seated upon clouds with red and green cloths beneath them like discarded clothing. One man turns to face the people behind him, like a man at the theater turning to greet old friends seated in the row behind him, while his other hand with its finger outstretched points to the figure of Jesus. The man beside him is reaching back to take the hand of a man in a turban. These are examples of figures who are frozen in the moment of meeting one another after death. Friends, old neighbors, loved ones find one another at the edge of eternal life.

Behind this group, is a cluster of faces that peek out from behind the figures standing in front of them. These faces, in various states of heightened emotion, grow dim in the distance, their features obscured in shadow and lacking the detail of the figures in front. Michelangelo is using a technique here that can be likened to a photographer's depth of field, in which there is an area of focus that can be seen clearly in the photograph while things that are outside that area are blurred. It is interesting to see it practiced here by Michelangelo, giving this sixteenth-century fresco a third dimension, one of infinite space stretching not just to the right and left, but also near and far.

If we accept that Michelangelo had intended this space to encompass an infinite distance in the direction of the wall, then it is safe to assume that the space also encompasses the Sistine Chapel and all those who stand before the fresco—who must then place themselves within the scene and ask themselves where their natural place would be. His use of ultramarine blue rather than vegetable dyes heightened this effect of infinite space, so that the sky of the *Last Judgment* is one of the most obvious differences between this later fresco and Michelangelo's vaulted ceiling.

Ultramarine blue, for all its beauty, is not the easiest pigment to work with, especially in fresco. For this reason, Michelangelo painted part of the work in fresco and part in tempera, which would allow him to modulate the color. Tempera is more fragile than fresco so the subtleties of color that Michelangelo intended were lost during centuries of cleaning. This is also true of some of the places in which Michelangelo had made corrections in a *secco* (as well as those censorious alterations made after his death). Most of the changes that he made to the *Last Judgment* were done to alter the position or dramatic pose of the characters, unlike the changes made in the vault, which were done to solve problems of perspective.

Scattered throughout the fresco are agents of judgment, angels to assist in the rise of the righteous and the fall of the damned. In the central group, seven angels are blowing trumpets or are preparing to do so. "The seven angels with the seven trumpets made ready to blow them."[7] The trumpets, of course, announce the presence of Christ and the Day of Judgment. Displaying all of the prejudice of the Renaissance world, the angels all have blonde hair, most with godlike curls, and all are well muscled. One angel at the top, wrapped in a green mantle, blows his horn vigorously, his eyes open wide, pupils directed to the right as if watching his fellow angels, like a singer in a choir trying to keep on beat. Beside him is another angel, arm outstretched to the back as if balancing himself, one knee propped on a cloud, and he is leaning forward with a long trumpet, blowing for all he is worth.

Interestingly enough, the balancing hand seems to be resting on the wall, his fingers splayed out as if he is leaning against it for support. The angel beside him is leaning forward as if speaking to the angel just below him who is preparing to blow his trumpet. His finger is pointing at the angel in the front of the group slightly to the left, who holds a small book and directs the open pages to the dead rising from their graves to seek a place among the elect. Beside him in an ochre mantle, another angel holds a much larger book toward those falling into damnation. Whether this larger book is a book of the damned is a subject of contention.

Catholic tradition does not mention a book listing the damned, only a book of the elect, the book of life. This is Christian iconography at its best. The small book is the book of life while the big book is pointed at the condemned. This seems to indicate that in Michelangelo's view more people are damned than are saved, even though he allocates far more space on the wall for the elect than for the damned.

The number of the elect versus the number of the damned is part of an old debate within Christendom. If you met someone on the street in Florence at the height of the Renaissance and asked him whether more people were saved than damned, he would say that more were saved by the mercy of God, which is overflowing with salvation. But if fifty years later you were to meet that same person on the streets of Florence, after the Sack of Rome and the siege of Florence, that person might, in good Catholic Reformation style, say that more people are damned than are saved. This ratio changed dramatically over the centuries, depending upon cultural and social conditions. Before the Black Death, images of Jesus as the good shepherd carrying a lamb over his shoulders was fairly common, but after the fourteenth century and the catastrophe of the plague, such images were less common, and the sense of God's judgment was stronger than the sense of God's mercy. This attitude swing seems to depend more upon what we think of ourselves than what we think of God. In fact, it might be argued that the real question of faith in the modern world is more the result of diminishing expectations about the place of humanity in the universe than it is about the psychology of God.

To the left of the trumpet blowing angels are a group of angels assisting more tepid souls to rise into the heavens. This hints at a Catholic distinction between fervent and tepid souls, those who are aflame with religious passion and those who are lukewarm. On the right side of this group is an angel with ginger-colored hair standing on a cloud and leaning over to haul two souls on to the cloud like fish. In good

Catholic fashion, he is using a rosary-like a rope, indicating to all those Catholics viewing the fresco that the rosary is a good way to get to heaven, and a statement about the value of intercessory prayer.

It is difficult to tell the angels from the saints, because Michelangelo has abandoned the traditional iconography of angels with wings. In that tradition, angels are asexual, but with vaguely male features, a simpering face, and hands clasped in prayer, watching over the travails of the human race. Michelangelo's angels, on the other hand, are more like muscular heroes or laboring men bending to the task. To the left of the angel hauling souls onto the cloud, there is another man also seated on a cloud, turning to watch some action that is happening behind him. This is probably not an angel but a soul who has attained the first level in his climb toward heaven because behind him in shadow is another figure who holds him around the waist as if he has just hauled him onto the cloud. Beside him are two dark skinned figures, with the woman behind hauling a man up onto the cloud. The man's eyes are wide and he is looking upward as if to say, "Don't drop me."

Interestingly, the variation in skin tone found among the figures in the *Last Judgment* may well reflect the same variation that existed in Renaissance Italy at the time, which indicates that there may well have been a sizable population of people of African descent in Europe even then. There had been human traffic between Europe and Africa for millennia. Some of this traffic had been part of a slave trade, which had been growing exponentially since the discovery of the New World. However, these people were not necessarily slaves although slaves did exist in Italy and throughout Europe; the difference between slaves and freemen was not drawn along racial lines at the time. We know that Alessandro de Medici, the first Duke of Tuscany and the illegitimate son of Clement VII, had an African mother and was the first man of mixed blood to hold such a rank in European society.

Surrounding these darker figures, is a group of people, some with blond hair, some naked, some dressed, reaching out their hands to lift a climbing soul onto a cloud. Just above the group with the angel hauling the two figures with a rosary is a small group of figures shadowed by distance and leaning over a cloud, hands extended like survivors on a lifeboat reaching out to save someone in the water. Their faces are full of tension, as if they are straining to assist this climbing soul, and as if they fear that he may sink like a drowning man without their help. This assistance of one soul by another is characteristic of the saved and is an instance of traditional Christian iconography. The difference between the saved and the damned is not so much freedom from the body as it is the willingness to help those in need.

Thus, throughout the history of Christian spirituality, there has been a tension between the Gnostic belief that salvation comes from release of the soul from the body and the Christian belief that salvation comes through the love of God and love of neighbor. These two great commandments, according to Jesus, are the summation of the Mosaic Law—that we should love God with all our heart, all our soul, all our mind, and all our strength, and that we should love our neighbor as ourselves.

The Gnostic belief all too often creates nothing but sadness and a sense of despair, for who can be free of the body while in the body? This was the great terror that beset Michelangelo in his later years. The Christian belief, if practiced, gives peace and a feeling of connection, traditional marks of salvation. According to Ignatius of Loyola, who knew Michelangelo and asked him to design the church of the Gesu, the central church of the Jesuit order, and who gave his followers rules for discernment, rules for knowing whether you are moving toward God or away from God; that is, rules for understanding the psychological movements of the heart, and what these movements mean.[8] For Ignatius, the first of these rules is that anything that leads you to God gives peace and serenity and anything that leads you away from God creates agitation in the soul.

The entire assembly of figures in the *Last Judgment* are reflections of Michelangelo's spiritual insecurity, as well as an expression of his Catholic Reformation theology. The central theological question of the fresco is, "Where will you be at the end of time, as all humanity is judged?" This was a prime existential concern for Michelangelo, who feared the answer to that question. It is this very uncertainty that characterized the Counter-Reformation, as a reaction to the relative complacency of the Renaissance. The positive humanism of the Renaissance deadened the medieval sense of sin, which rebounded in the Counter-Reformation.

Artistically, Michelangelo's *Last Judgment* is a solidly Renaissance work. Theologically, however, it springs from his long association with the Catholic reform movement, from Savonarola to the Council of Trent. It is ironic that the same reform movement produced a prudish, reactionary spirituality that would eventually condemn the *Last Judgment* as obscene, for reasons that had more to do with the reform movement's rejection of the Renaissance than its rejection of the theology embodied in the fresco.

Chapter Ten

The Outer Orbit: The Naked and the Dead

I saw the dead, the great and the lowly, standing before the throne, and scrolls were opened, another scroll was opened, the book of life. The dead were judged according to their deeds, by what was written in the scrolls. The sea gave up its dead; then Death and Hades gave up their dead. All the dead were judged according to their deeds. Then Death and Hades were thrown into the pool of fire (this pool of fire is the second death.) Anyone whose name was not found written in the book of life was thrown into the pool of fire.

—Revelations 20:12–15

The human drama in the *Last Judgment* begins with the dead. In the lower left corner of the fresco, a group of people are climbing out of their graves. Some are mere skeletons, while others still retain the flesh of the living. In the middle of this group, a man crouches with one foot on the ground and one foot in the grave. His head is turned to the right where an angel and a demon are struggling over two souls, one upright and fully clothed in a green mantle and the other upside down and naked. The angel holds the inverted man by his legs while the demon pulls on his hair. Though they struggle to rise to heaven, the fact that the angels are assisting them in their flight indicates that they are among the elect. The angels on the right side, for example, pummel the damned from above, forcing them into the underworld, for they can no longer be saved. To the left of this tug of war is the half-naked figure of a man wrapped in a white pall. He is being lifted into the sky by a young man, perhaps an angel, who grasps him under the arms and pulls him skyward. Unlike some of the other bodies climbing out of the grave, this man's skin is gray, still wearing the coloring of death. He too is being attacked from below by a demon whose hand is the only visible part of him, rising out of a hole in the earth and wrapping a green snake around the man's legs.

This image of angels and demons struggling over human souls comes out of an ancient tradition, pre-dating Dante, but expressed admirably in his poetry. The world is seen as a battlefield between good and evil. The angels, the soldiers of good, struggle to carry the souls to heaven, while the demons, the soldiers of evil, struggle to drag the souls to hell. This vision of the world has its roots outside Christianity, in Manichaeism, a late variant of Zoroastrianism. In these religious systems, originally from Persia and Afghanistan, there are two sets of gods—the light and the dark. In Manichaeism, the god of good, the Good Principle, rules the heavens and is called the Father of Majesty or Greatness, Megethos, or Abba D'rabbutha. He is the source of order and peace. Eternally opposed to him is the King of Darkness, who lives in the world below—including this world, the world of matter—and is inversely dark and evil. Manichaeism snuck into Christianity early on, during the first five centuries, and mixed with Jewish apocalyptic visions of the children of light and darkness inherited by the nascent church.

To the left of the man with the grey skin and toward the back, a man is being cradled by a skeleton, almost tenderly, as if he had once been family. As the dead rise, their bodies are re-formed, their flesh gathering around their bones. Some in the scene have finished this process, while others are merely skeletons, awaiting the flesh. The man is lying on a skull that has a casket pillow and shroud underneath it. His eyes are closed as if he has not yet awakened. The skeleton is looking in the direction of the trumpeting angels. The fact that he is still a skeleton does not necessarily mean that he is one of the damned, only that there are stages in resurrection. As Saint Augustine wrote, it would be foolish to think that the Creator of all would be incapable of assembling our bodies and bringing them back to life. The Creator could do it even if our bodies had been eaten by beasts or consumed in fire.[1]

With this group, the great rotation begins. The souls rising from the dead fly upward, or try to, where they will live among the elect or fall once again into damnation. The souls move like planets around the person of Christ, who shines like the sun. All are drawn to him as if by a divine gravitation. The Copernican universe had been turned into religious art. Very few people during Michelangelo's time noticed this, partly because *de Revolutionibus* would not be published for another ten years. Even in Galileo's time, when the Copernican universe was on trial, it appears that no one noticed Michelangelo's allusion to Copernicus.[2] If they had, it would surely have inflamed the reactionary elements of the Catholic Reformation and led to a renewed call for the fresco's destruction. Michelangelo's critics, concerned about decorum, were too busy complaining about the nudity in the fresco to notice that he had encoded in the painting an idea that would change the world.

Following Michelangelo's path, left to right, right to left, as he created the fresco, this is the last group to be painted. The resurrection group has 41 figures and it took Michelangelo 35 days to finish it. The very last person to be painted was a small figure on the extreme lower left corner, peeking out of his grave.[3] Unlike many of the other sections of the fresco, this section was painted almost entirely in *buon' fresco* with very few changes.

A noteworthy problematic area in the fresco was the foot of the man being dragged into the sky by an angel in a red robe, with a demon reaching up from a hole in the earth, wrapping a snake around his legs, trying to pull him back. Michelangelo obsessively revised this foot *a secco,* as well as other elements in the figure including the serpent, the demon's hand, and the angel's red robe. The cartoons for this section were transferred by indirect engraving in some areas, and by pouncing in others, with black marks drawn along the perforations prior to painting. The small figures in the background, who are looking skyward, seem to have been painted quickly, without a cartoon. As Michelangelo hastened to finish the project, he began working faster and more confidently, and in many areas he skipped the outlining step to apply the pigments spontaneously.

Painting this section marked a difficult time for Michelangelo, because the depiction touched on his own spiritual demons. He reacted the way that he usually did, by retreating into his solitude and snarling at anyone who tried to draw him out of it. He had always swaddled himself in his work, but that necessary solitude was never healthy, and he often grew depressed. This irritable, antisocial behavior exhibited itself in his persistent determination not to forgive Sebastiano del Piombo for preparing the wall for oil painting, and in his refusal to see his nephew Lionardo who wanted to come visit him in Rome, complaining that the visit would merely add to his burdens.

Michelangelo's conception of the end of time was traditional. The Fourth Lateran Council in 1215, a council of bishops convoked by Pope Innocent III, declared that all humanity, righteous people and sinners, would rise again, and that their bodies would be incorruptible—that is, they could not die. Those who belonged to the elect would possess four transcendent endowments: *impassibility,* which meant that they could not suffer; *glory,* which meant their bodies would shine like the sun; *agility,* which meant that they would not be constrained by the limitations of space but would be able to be in whatever place they wished to be; and *subtility,*[4] which meant that their souls would be in complete control of their bodies. The damned would have no such qualities, and while they could no longer die, they could suffer. Their bodies would be darkened like shadows, and they would be limited by space just as they were when they were alive. The bodies of the damned would dominate them and become a source of torment for them.[5] Michelangelo's use of this theology could date back to his years listening to Savonarola, a Dominican friar like Thomas Aquinas who adapted the doctrine from the Fourth Lateran Council for his monumental *Summa Theologica,* which summarizes the reasoning behind most points of Western Christian theology.[6]

The *Last Judgment* fresco contained no new theological ideas but was an expression of traditional Catholic theology. Even though he might have discussed religion, philosophy, and even theology with his friends, Michelangelo was not formally educated in these things and did not believe that he was a qualified authority. For him, the general resurrection of the dead was a certainty—all would awaken on the last day and would rise with their own bodies. The spiritual bodies that they would receive were actually perfect versions of their human forms and not entirely new appearances. Because he believed this so strongly, every figure that he painted in the *Last Judgment* was an expression of his faith. Each figure played a part in the theological story of the end of the world. Michelangelo believed this story wholeheartedly, and imagined details that fit it and painted them into his fresco.

We must admit, however, that the resurrection of the body is a strange idea. It stands somewhere between reincarnation and the immortality of the soul. Right from the beginning, when Saint Paul proclaimed it to the people of Athens, most of them mocked him, for nothing could be stranger to the classical Greek mind than the idea of returning to your own flesh. Plato believed that the body was an irritant, something that got in the way of philosophy. The philosopher was lucky to be rid of it in death.

The idea that the dead shall awaken and reinhabit their old flesh is what makes the Christian doctrine of the resurrection of the body so unusual. In their opposition between body and spirit, the Gnostics went so far as to deny that Jesus actually had a body. They believed that during the crucifixion, the suffering Jesus was not the real one but a fake, and that the real Jesus, who is pure spirit, was hovering overhead laughing at the foolishness of those who would seek to cause him pain, for as a pure spirit he was completely free of such bindings.[7] The Christian tradition, on the other hand, is rooted in the Jewish tradition and in the writings of Saint Paul, and refuses to back away from the oddness of the resurrection of the body, where the dead rise into their original bodies, even though those bodies may have been buried for thousands of years. The Christian tradition, refuses to idealize the resurrection, refuses to make it something that is figurative, or to make it a metaphor not to be taken literally. It is just that literalness that is at the heart of Michelangelo's fresco. There is a great deal of symbolic power in the painting, but that symbolism is more of an expression of Michelangelo's faith in the reality of the resurrection than a subversion of it.

The advantage of the resurrection of the body is that it is completely human. It would it be hard to imagine a spirit floating around for all eternity, a disembodied mind. To be human is to have a body, but on the Day of Judgment those bodies are no longer subject to death or disease, but are incorruptible, to be sent whole to either heaven or hell. This would apply not only to the blessed but to the damned. For the blessed this is a source of joy, but for the damned, imagining a lifetime of corporeal suffering in hell, is a source of torment. If one accepts the idea of resurrection, one would expect the dead to rise unclothed. The new resurrected flesh does not imply a wardrobe, nor should it, for the resurrection of the body should imply a return to the state of innocence that Adam and Eve had in the garden.

Nudity was not a problem for Michelangelo as it would be for many of his critics. What mattered to Michelangelo was the one question that Michelangelo did not and could not raise in his fresco. How did one become a member of the elect? This is the ultimate insecurity of the faithful, the question that nags every believer. Am I faithful enough?

No one has ever had an answer for this, and maybe that is why this question, which sparked so much insecurity, was the cause of such terrible dissention, even warfare, between Catholics and Protestants. It was the most loaded theological question of the sixteenth and seventeenth centuries. John Calvin in Geneva was arguing, in a strict interpretation of Saint Augustine, that election was predestined, a part of God's eternal plan, and that human beings did not possess free will but were simply corks floating on the divine sea. Anything other than that would limit the omnipotence of God. This was a harsh doctrine, and nearly everyone, Catholics and Protestants alike, except Calvin's immediate followers, rejected it. Even Calvinists eventually found ways around this doctrine because it was a kind of fatalism that preached that it didn't matter what one did in life or believed in life, because your fate had been decided before you were born. This doctrine placed God's omnipotence above all, but in doing so, it made his choice in drawing up the list of the elect seem almost capricious.

In a way, membership in the elect or inclusion among the damned is just as mysterious in the *Last Judgment* fresco, for there is no real inkling given in the artwork that demonstrates why some are saved and others damned. The only biblical reference is in Matthew 25, in the passage where the good are divided like sheep from goats, and the one rule by which they would be separated was whether they had reached out in love to assist those who needed it. "As long as you do this to one of these, my least brothers and sisters, you do it to me," says the Son of God in the act of judgment. In Michelangelo's fresco, all humanity waits in fear and trembling as the judgment is pronounced.

CHAPTER ELEVEN

The Damned

On the lower right hand side of Michelangelo's *Last Judgment,* the figure called the reprobate falls toward hell, caught in the moment of realization that he has lived a lie, that his life had been one of sin, and that he belongs in hell. One hand half covers his face, as if he cannot look at what is about to happen to him. Still, he must watch and his exposed features are clenched with horror—the one exposed eye is wide, dreading everything it sees. He is terrified. His emotions are so stark, so powerful because he seems to be awakening to a truth about himself that he had long denied. In this sense, he is everyman, finally forced to look at his true self and hating what he sees.

Two demons tug at the reprobate's feet, one grabbing him around his calves and the other holding on to one foot, swinging there like dead weight to bring him down. A green snake wraps around his leg and bites him in the thigh. He is a morally unprincipled person, shameless, one who has rejected God by living in sin, one who is rejected by God and without hope of salvation. Michelangelo does not reveal what led him to this state, for he depicts him in the instant of realization, the instant of judgment. Perhaps he is there because of his own actions, because he has lived a shameless life, or he is there because of some mysterious turn of fate, according to Calvin the unfathomable will of God had predestined him for damnation even before his birth.

To the right of this figure, a group of doomed souls struggles to fight their way up to heaven, or to stay out of hell. The angels are not there to help them rise, but to pummel them down to their proper place. There is one man in the group, a naked figure upside down, with a set of keys and a bag of gold tied to his chest. A demon has him by the throat and is dragging him down. The viewer is led to wonder if these are the keys of Peter, which would make him an avaricious pope who loved gold more than God, a bad shepherd who misused spiritual power. This perhaps was Michelangelo's most visible condemnation of the luxurious lifestyle of the popes and ecclesiastics.

Above him, an angel in an ocher-colored tunic pushes him toward hell with one hand and has the other raised in a fist as for a punch. To the right of him is another figure, this time standing upright. An angel floats above him and appears ready to strike him in the face. The two grapple with each other like wrestlers, the damned trying to grab hold of the angel to keep from falling and the angel trying to shove him down. Between these two figures is a man wrapped in a long white shroud covering most of his head, falling face first toward the abyss, his hands clasped in prayer. Is he praying to God for his release, or is he begging the demons all-around not to harm him? At the extreme right of the group is a man in a shroud that is coming undone. His back is to the viewer but his face has turned, revealing a stark white eye and his hand stuffed into his mouth to stop him from screaming. Directly beneath him is a demon who seems to be pulling on the man's testicles. Michelangelo hints in this depiction that this man's sin is of a sexual nature.

There is another man on the left side of the fresco opposite the damned in the group of those who have newly arisen; he too is being tugged by a demon with horns. But in this case, there is also an angel above him pulling him toward heaven. This the difference between one who is damned because of unrepented sin and one who has repented but is still weighed down by the flesh. This is the Catholic distinction between the damned and those who must go to purgatory. The people in purgatory are saved but unclean. They must go through a period of purgation through suffering that will purify them and make them ready to join the elect. Catholic tradition, then, defines two periods of judgment: the particular judgment that happens immediately after death and the general judgment that happens at the end of the world. Those who are damned have died with a personal mortal sin on their souls. According to Thomas Aquinas, a mortal sin is one which kills the grace of God in the soul, and so when you die in such a state you have no place to go but hell. Those who repent, either through a perfect act of contrition or through the sacrament of penance feel the grace of God flowing back into them. At the base of the judgment then, the Catholic tradition states that people go to hell because of their own actions and their own choices. There is no predestination, as with Calvin, except in the most vague sense of the term, since God knows what you will choose and allows you to choose it.

For the group of sinners on the right side of the fresco—the one with the bag of gold and keys and the one who is being dragged to hell by his testicles—we see Michelangelo coming down on the side of the Catholic tradition. The fate of these figures is clearly linked to their mortal sins. However, in the case of the reprobate, Michelangelo gives no such insight and leaves us to imagine the nature of his sin. In this, he seems to be favoring the new Protestant ideas from Germany and Switzerland, ideas that he had encountered through Vittoria Colonna. As far as the viewer can see, the reprobate has no symbol of his sin, yet is labeled as a sinner because he is in the group that is falling to hell. The reprobate, however, may be one who does not believe, and the nature of his horror is to find out that he had been wrong about God and the afterlife, about heaven and hell. Michelangelo thus demonstrates two opposing visions of salvation and damnation. These visions were very much alive in his time, as they are today. The Protestant view is stated simply: We are all justified by faith alone, and those who believe in Jesus as the Christ will be saved. The Catholic view is a bit more complex. While Catholics believe that we are justified by faith, it is that little word "alone" that creates a distinction: Catholics believe that there are two components to salvation—faith and good works. It is not enough to simply believe—one's faith must make one reach out and help alleviate the suffering of one's neighbors. It is possible that the man with the bag of gold was a true believer, but because of his avarice, faith alone did not stop him from going to hell.

The problem with the Catholic view is that if good works are necessary as well as faith, one never knows if they have done enough. The answer is that, of course, you have not done enough—you will never do enough. And so salvation comes from the power of God and from faith in it, which leads us back to the Protestant camp. The distinction between these two camps, therefore, is often a matter of perspective. Neither is logically complete, and the disparity between the Protestant and Catholic versions of salvation is as much a matter of emphasis as of a real difference.

There are 25 figures in the group of damned souls to the right of the trumpeters, and it took Michelangelo 30 days to paint them. They were painted in *buon' fresco,* but a number of areas have been painted *a secco:* for example, one of the demons dragging the reprobate has been retouched several times. The cartoon was transferred here by indirect engraving. One of the demons grabbing onto the reprobate contains an error that Michelangelo did not catch and retouch *a secco:* his hand is the color of human skin instead of gray-green like the rest of his body.

In 1534, while Michelangelo was painting this group of figures, Pope Paul came to visit him, bringing along the papal master of ceremonies, Biagio da Cesena. Cesena was a precise man, with regular habits and a deep concern about the rules of form. While Michelangelo looked on, Pope Paul asked Cesena what he thought of the fresco. Cesena responded that he didn't like it at all, that it seemed improper to be painting all of that nudity on the wall of the Sistine Chapel, and that it was a dishonor to the site. Then he said that such pictures were better suited for roadside taverns or bath houses.[1]

Michelangelo was furious, and when the two of them left, he decided that he would have his revenge. As soon as they were gone, he drew Cesena's likeness from memory and placed the master of ceremonies among the damned in hell as the figure of Minos, the judge of the damned. He gave him donkey's ears and wound a large green snake around his legs that had its head firmly attached to his penis. Surrounding him was an army of devils. When he saw this, Biagio Cesena was horrified and he entreated Michelangelo to remove the portrait, but the artist refused. Then he went to Pope Paul and asked him to order Michelangelo to do so, but Pope Paul, thinking the whole thing was very funny, said, "Had Michelangelo sent you to Purgatory, I could intercede for you. But since he has placed you in hell, I have no power to save you."

The figure of Minos is painted in the extreme lower right-hand corner of the fresco amid a troop of demons in the shape of male figures with horns. They await a boatload of the damned who have just run aground on a protruding rock and are leaping and being dragged from the boat by the demons. The leading figure, apparently the first off the boat, has his hands in fists, ready to fight. Another man behind him leans over as if to grab hold of a demon. There are no signs here of mutual assistance or even of teamwork. The damned souls leaving the ship are a mob, all screaming, some shrinking away from the demons, others readying to fight them. Minos, even with the snake wrapped around him, seems to be watching impassively as the damned souls leap from the boat. A dark-skinned soul directly behind Minos is pointing to the boat. His eyes are wide as if he fears the coming of the damned. Michelangelo has caught him in the middle of giving a report, as to a general on a battlefield. He took these images from Canto V of Dante's *Inferno:*

> Minos stands there, snarling
> Examines the sins at the entrance
> Judges and commands him on as he girds him
> I say that when the spirit born to sin
> Comes before him, tells him all
> And this analyst of transgression
> Knows his rightful place in Hell
> Coils his tail the number of times
> The levels he wants the soul to be thrown down.[2]

Michelangelo was an avid reader of Dante's works and, according to Condivi, he had read the *Divine Comedy* every night for nearly a year.[3] Whether this is an exaggeration or not we will never know, but we do know that Dante filled Michelangelo with images of hell and heaven. As a poet, Michelangelo wrote a number of poems in praise of Dante whom he greatly admired; as a sculptor, he had long desired to carve a monument in Florence as a memorial to its greatest literary genius.

Dante had also been deeply interested in astronomy and cosmology, although it was a strictly Aristotelian universe that he described. His levels in hell, purgatory, and heaven were all perfect circles in good Aristotelian fashion, and they formed three distinct hierarchies. Dante himself had been deeply influenced by Thomas Aquinas, who was Christianity's great interpreter of Aristotle. It is not difficult to believe that Michelangelo had already developed an interest in astronomy and cosmology before he painted the *Last Judgment,* and that he had developed that interest by his reading of Dante.

The figure of Minos was taken by Dante directly from Greek mythology. As an early Renaissance writer, his poetry was a combination of Christian theology and classical imagery. This is one of the reasons why Michelangelo chose to put Minos into his vision of hell, or at least the portal to hell. This grouping that depicted both Minos and Charon was Michelangelo's tribute to his favorite poet, and some scholars see in their presence the possibility of a key to understanding his structure of the *Last Judgment.* There have been some attempts to identify each of the figures in the fresco with characters in the poem, and some of these efforts have been forced. But there is some truth to the idea that Michelangelo was so imbued with Dante's verbal images of hell and heaven that he consciously designed much of the fresco to dovetail with Dante's poem.

Charon, the second major character in this group, was described by Dante as the gatekeeper of the River Styx and the ferryman who carried the damned across the river of death to the land of the dead. In Greek mythology, everyone went to Hades because it was the place of the dead. Tartarus was the place of punishment, and for the Greeks the truly damned were sent there. The Elysian fields were the place for good souls. In Christian mythology, however, Hades was the place reserved for the wicked, while the just would be brought up into the heavens to live with God forever, as described by Saint Paul. Dante's description of hell closely follows that Christian division but illustrated with Christian imagery. Charon the ferryman, as depicted by both Dante and Michelangelo, is no longer the demigod who must be paid to allow the soul to enter Hades;

> Look here! Coming toward us in a boat
> an ancient man, white with age
> "Woe to you, sinful souls!" he cries

"Give up hope to see the sky
I will take you to the other side
To darkness without end, in fire and ice
You there! Living soul standing there
Back away from this lot, who are all dead."
But when he saw that I did not withdraw
He said "Go round by other ways, by other ports
To that far shore, but don't come here for passage
A lighter vessel must carry you."[4]

To the left of the Minos group, Michelangelo painted the mouth of hell. This is the only place in the entire fresco where the spectator gets a peek at either heaven or hell. His treatment here is reminiscent of his famous cartoon for the Battle of Cascina, which he had drawn years before for a competition with Leonardo da Vinci to paint a fresco on the government house in Florence. In his cartoon, he caught a group of soldiers bathing in a stream, just before the battle. The horns have sounded in the distance, and the men are glancing up, recognizing that the time had come for war. Michelangelo caught the power of that balancing moment, not the moment of battle but the moment just before.

Michelangelo's treatment of the last judgment is similar. He depicts the Day of Judgment, the moment of separation, not the final fate of those being judged. He does not show heaven, only the place where Jesus appears and where judgment begins. He shows hell only through this tiny window of the cave. At the mouth of the cave are two apelike demons, hiding in the shadows, waiting to waylay anyone who comes in their direction. One has his mouth open wide, revealing great flat teeth. He is not snarling, however, for his mouth is open in astonishment, and his eyes are wide, the pupils directed slightly upward, as if he is listening to the trumpets. Beside these two figures is the figure of a man, his back to the spectator, his arms out before him as if feeling the heat. Some scholars have speculated that this is a second self portrait of Michelangelo, depicting himself just before he enters the second death of hell. There are no self-portraits in the fresco showing Michelangelo among the Elect, except as an empty, flayed skin. His sense of his own sinfulness was a terrible burden to him, coming out repeatedly in his poetry and his painting.

This image of the cave was carefully designed for its position directly over the main altar of the chapel because Michelangelo had a dark view of the popes as the result of all the years that he lived in Rome and worked in and around the papal court. The popes were corrupt, tyrannical, and power mad and as the chapel was primarily used by the pope and his household and court, this message of condemnation was aimed at them.

That his art could have a message and a functionality placed him in agreement with the approach of the Catholic Reformation, which began to see art as instructional rather than the Renaissance view that it was something that existed for its own sake. Michelangelo saw in his *Last Judgment* an opportunity to do for the pope what Savonarola could not do, that is, to speak directly to him and to his household, to prophesy to them and warn them of the coming perdition. This is why he painted the damned soul with the money bag and two keys, which are remarkably like the same keys that Peter is offering Jesus in the center ring of the fresco. Because the keys of the kingdom are the symbol of Peter and of the papacy in general, they act as an iconographic marker, identifying the soul as a deceased pope. Again, this was a chance to make a point to the papal court, a point that he believed was long overdue.

When Michelangelo was busy painting the group of soaring bodies halfway up the left side of the fresco, on approximately the same level as the falling pope with the keys on the other side, he fell off the scaffolding, and badly hurt his leg. In his pain and embarrassment, he retreated like a wounded animal to his house and locked himself in, refusing to see a physician, refusing to let any of his friends come and help him. It is likely that the painting of the *Last Judgment* was beginning to affect him and with this wound, he retreated irrationally from the world, even to the point of endangering his health.

A Florentine physician, Maestro Baccio Rontini, who was a friend and admirer of Michelangelo's and quite used to his eccentricities, went to Michelangelo's house to see if he could help. He knocked on the door, but no one answered, not even a servant. He went to one of the neighbor's houses and received no reply there either. But as a friend of Michelangelo's he knew of the secret entrance around the back, and tiptoeing from room to room he finally arrived where Michelangelo lay wounded, in a desperate state.[5] When Michelangelo tried to demand that he leave, Rontini refused and, while Vasari does not mention how long Michelangelo's convalescence was, from that moment on, Rontini never left his bedside until his leg had healed. Michelangelo was in his mid-60s at this time and his natural bodily strength wasn't what it had been.

After his recovery, he returned to the Sistine Chapel, to the Minos group, and then finished the rest of the fresco in the next few months. He refused to take pity on the donkey-eared Cesena and let the portrait stand.[6]

CHAPTER TWELVE

The Censorship of the
End of the World

*I*n 1541, Michelangelo finished the *Last Judgment.* All of the revisions were complete, the touchups, the repositioning of hands and arms, the *a secco* additions and corrections. The fresco had taken him five years to accomplish and in that time he had succumbed several times to depression, retreating ever farther into his solitude and growing ever more irascible. Pope Paul III set the date, Christmas Day, to swing open the doors of the Sistine Chapel to reveal the new fresco to the world. He had already had a private viewing with his staff and cardinals when he celebrated a mass on All Saints' Eve in October of that year. People all over Europe had been anticipating this fresco which they thought would be the culmination of Michelangelo's career. Letters, articles, and poetry praising this new work circulated around Italy even before the fresco was finished, written by people who had not even seen it.

People remembered the amazement the Romans felt when they saw Michelangelo's magnificent ceiling two decades earlier. Everyone had praised it and said it was the finest work ever done. So on Christmas Day, 1541, when the doors opened and the pope's guests trooped inside to gaze at the new fresco, the reaction was not what Michelangelo expected. To be sure, many people praised it, saying it was the finest work of its kind and the obvious high point of Michelangelo's career. His supporters said that the *Last Judgment* made celestial figures larger than life and more beautiful than they would be in nature. Ascanio Condivi, Michelangelo's personally chosen biographer, loved it, calling it sublime."[1] Giorgio Vasari, Michelangelo's other contemporary biographer, in 1550, wrote that the fresco's details and the number of figures expresses the entire range of human emotion."[2]

Michelangelo's supporters saw the fresco as the height of Renaissance art. But just as many, perhaps even more, thought that it was the work of an arrogant man, a man whose artistry had become hubris. There seemed to be too much art and not enough religion, which would have worked in the Renaissance but not in the Counter-Reformation.[3] On the side, people made obscene jokes about the nudes.

One Venetian comic writer, Andrea Calmo, wrote that Michelangelo had earned praise for his work not only from God and from other artists, but also from demigods, nymphs, satyrs, philosophers, astrologers, poets, magicians. People were both horrified and fascinated with the figures of Saint Catherine and Saint Blaise. Gradually, the criticisms began to outweigh the praise. There were philosophers and poets among the critics, many of whom saw their critiques as an opportunity to get their words in print. Michelangelo's universal fame had become a lightning rod. Extended critiques built upon each other, setting up a literary conversation about art, religion, and decorum. The intended audience for these critiques was no longer the tight in-group at the Vatican; at this point, their audience was the wider public, who could not see the fresco as it was painted in the chapel but could buy prints made of copies drawn by other less-accomplished (but nonetheless fairly accurate) artists.

This wider audience was not the group for whom Michelangelo had painted the *Last Judgment,* nor did he expect that these people would ever see it. He had painted the fresco for the usual inhabitants of the Sistine Chapel—the pope and his *famiglia,* his household and his staff. The size of this group varied under each pope. Pope Leo X had over 700 advisers, bureaucrats, servants, secretaries, footmen, coachmen and entertainers working for him in the papal palace; Pope Paul III's household was significantly smaller.

The members of Michelangelo's imagined audience were there-fore all part of the same elite group: mostly clergy and a few laymen, usually strictly males, who were permitted to attend ceremonies at the Sistine Chapel. Many of them were well-educated in matters of theol-ogy and art, and were sophisticated in their ability to understand the subtleties of artistic creations. They would see that the *Last Judgment* had a unique purpose and set up a unique relationship with them as the audience.

Michelangelo's fresco involved the spectator in ways that tra-ditional last judgments did not. In the fresco, the dead rose from their tombs as a group, but in the process of judgment they were separated as individuals, never to see each other again. The intended audience knew that Michelangelo's goal was not to paint some long-ago-and-faraway scene, something that happened to someone else who was no longer alive. They would understand that the fresco was about some-thing that would happen eventually, something that would involve the audience as well, something that they could not escape.

Papal masses were a bit like theater, but their performance was not for an audience. The papal household—mostly cardinals, bish-ops, and priests—would gather in the Sala Regia in strict order, according to their rank in the household, before entering the chapel. This order was compared to the celestial hierarchy which, during the sermons, they were often encouraged to look up at—that is, at the ceiling—and see the ranks of heaven that they represented on earth.

Pictorial last judgments, however, were traditionally meant to remind the viewers of the ultimate triumph of the church. Michelangelo's work did not fulfill these expectations, because he did not depict the apostles enthroned around the person of Christ. Rather, he depicted them without their usual vestments and signs of rank in a sort of loose crowd, without order or control. Instead of standing back waiting for Peter to speak, they seem to all speak at once, trying to catch Christ's attention.

Moreover, Michelangelo did not use the symbols of office in the traditional way. It was customary to show Saint Peter holding the keys to the kingdom and trying to return them to Christ since his office had been fulfilled. The keys to the kingdom were symbolic of spiritual authority, a symbol of the power of the priesthood, most particularly of the papacy, that "whatever you declare bound on earth shall be bound in heaven, whatever you declare loosed on earth shall be loosed in heaven."[4] However, Michelangelo had also displayed the keys to the kingdom in another area of the fresco, hanging around the neck of one of the damned who was falling into hell. There was a little sermon intended here for the eyes of the church elite, because along with the keys to the kingdom the damned soul had a bag of gold suspended from his neck. This was a reversal worthy of Dante and was a strictly reformist move on Michelangelo's part, warning the powerful of the Catholic Church that with their power came responsibilities and not just privileges.

One of the accusations leveled against the *Last Judgment* was that it was inappropriate and that it lacked proper decorum. This is what Biagio da Cesena, Pope Paul III's master of ceremonies, meant when he complained that the fresco properly belonged in a tavern. But the pope did not see it that way and accepted what Michelangelo had painted, seeing past the nudity to the theological heart of the fresco. For Michelangelo and his elite audience, decorum meant appropriateness, even visual consistency—for example, if you were going to paint an old man, you would not give him a young man's body. By painting perfect bodies on the resurrected dead Michelangelo, in his own view, had not broken with decorum, because one would expect that a perfect human, God's highest creation and achievement, would look perfect. This applied even to the damned, who in their physical perfection, that is, undying and free from disease, they would suffer more, for they would yearn for the ease of oblivion. Michelangelo and his intended audience would have used an artist's definition of decorum.[5]

The more sophisticated members of the papal household would have had no problems seeing a beardless Christ, nor would they have had problems with the vast array of nude figures. Moreover, they could see Michelangelo's association of the perfection of the body as a sign of the perfection of the soul. They would be able to catch Michelangelo's allusions to earlier works of art. For example, they would have connected the pose of the Virgin with the pose of the Crouching Venus, a Greek bronze from the third century BCE. In this sculpture, the goddess not only crouches but leans forward with her arms wrapped around her and her face turned away, much as the Virgin Mary is doing in Michelangelo's fresco. But they would also have seen a reference to Michelangelo's earlier Sistine Chapel ceiling fresco, the *Expulsion of Adam and Eve from Paradise,* in which Eve's hands are crossed over her breasts and her head is turned aside, much like with the Virgin Mary here. There Eve is disheveled and ugly, whereas the Mary in the *Last Judgment* is young and beautiful. Nevertheless, Michelangelo's audience would have understood the reference, because just as Jesus was called the second Adam, the one who healed what Adam had wounded, Mary was called the second Eve.

Few members of Michelangelo's intended audience would have been shocked by the fresco, because they understood the theology underlying the artistry. But surprisingly, some cardinals and members of Pope Paul's staff were shocked. Even while Michelangelo was painting the *Last Judgment,* his audience was changing and he had no control over this. Something new had entered the world—something that would change everything even more than the Copernican revolution. Michelangelo's fresco would no longer have to face only the probing eyes of the papal *famiglia,* it would have to face something new—public opinion, brought about by the printing press and its explosive effect on late Renaissance life. Several artists had begun to copy the fresco in engravings and, with the development and spread of the printing press, prints of these engravings circulated widely throughout Europe.

The first group to object to Michelangelo's new fresco was the Theatine order, one of the new religious orders that had emerged to work for the reform of the church. The order had been founded by Cardinal Cajetan and Cardinal Carafa who would later become the reactionary Pope Paul IV, the man most responsible for the Index of Forbidden Books and the creation of the Roman Jewish ghetto, and an avowed enemy of Ignatius Loyola and the Jesuits. The order was named after the city of Chiete (or Theate), a city of the Abruzzi in central Italy and the episcopal see of Carafa. The order had been approved on June 24, 1524, by Pope Clement VII, and Cajetan with his companions took their solemn vows in front of the papal altar at St. Peter's. The new order dedicated itself to improving the spiritual life of the clergy, and through them, to leading the laity into a new life of virtue and sanctity. The main focus of their ministry was to preach against Martin Luther and the other Protestants, and to try to bring the common people of Europe back to the true fold. The members of the order lived a very strict life and committed themselves to asceticism and poverty.

They were a highly conservative order, strict in their moralizing and severe in their demands upon the Christian soul but it was not their conservative views that were threatened by Michelangelo's *Last Judgment*. They were far more worried about its effects on the common layman, who would inevitably make up the wider audience as prints became available. They feared the depictions in the fresco would lure people away from piety. Even though Michelangelo had painted the fresco for the papal court, Pope Paul allowed other artists into the chapel to view the new work and to copy it. It was a daunting task, but many of them were able to copy the fresco closely enough to create reasonable facsimiles. Among the seventeen versions made during the sixteenth century, most notable was the one made by Marcello Venusti, a painter of second rank who was commissioned to make a miniature copy to send to the Duke of Urbino. It was good enough to survive through the years and many books today print his version rather than the original.[6]

The Theatine order was just one element in the growing pressure for reform. Pope Paul III had himself planned to call a great ecumenical council to address the growing Protestant movements and to promote reform within the church. He appointed Cardinal Contarini to head a tribunal to examine the needs for reform within the church. Meanwhile, there was a growing schism between the Spirituali and the more conservative elements in the church who became more interested in defending the Catholic Church against the Protestants. This reactionary wing would eventually dominate the coming reform.

At this point, Pietro Aretino reenters the picture. In a shameless second letter in 1537, he had pestered Michelangelo to send him a drawing from his own hand so that Aretino could show everyone in Venice what good taste he had, but Michelangelo never responded. Aretino, the "Scourge of Princes," did not like to be ignored.

After fleeing Rome, he took up residence in Venice, a traditional haven for troublemakers and eccentrics. From there, he wrote and published a series of satirical letters, sending them as obvious satire to the most important people of Europe. He addressed several letters to the Emperor Charles V, referring to him as Caesar and saying that he was to be praised for his righteousness, his piety, and his force of arms. Both the emperor and the king of France gave Aretino a pension because they wanted to use his poison pen to attack each other. Aretino made a small fortune on what we would call today blackmail, by offering not to publish some satire about a powerful person, or by hinting that without the proper gifts he might write such a satire. His attack on Michelangelo, however, was a bit more personal. It was also a great deal more opportunistic. Aretino's criticism of Michelangelo lasted longer than anyone else's, covering a longer time span. Within 13 years, his position on the fresco had changed and had become an ardent critic. In the intervening years, much had changed.

In 1545 Aretino sent his third letter on Michelangelo, a vicious attack not only upon the fresco but upon Michelangelo's character that hurt the brooding artist deeply. It is obvious that he did this out of personal pique because Michelangelo would not send him a drawing. But it is also true, and perhaps more true, that Aretino saw the changing mood in Italy and noted the growing audience for criticism of the fresco. He had never seen the fresco in the chapel, but he did see one of the many copies. At first he was excited about it. He even remarked that someone could make a great deal of money printing these and selling them to the public.[7] Michelangelo's fame was so great that everyone, from pope to peasant, wanted a little piece of his genius. The prints became an overnight success, but instead of increasing Michelangelo's fame, it increased his infamy. Aretino saw a literary opportunity, and after years of writing pornographic satires, he wrote a letter to Michelangelo that was filled with moralistic indignation:

> By placing art above faith, those who are Christian makes a spectacle by showing martyrs and virgins with such a lack of decorum. The look of the man who was grabbed by his testicles makes one avert his eyes to avoid seeing it, just as if one were standing in a brothel. Faith that is expressed in such a way that it undermines the faith of others is more sinful than atheism.[8]

This letter was specifically written to wound Michelangelo in every sore spot he could. It ridiculed him for his solitary lifestyle, attacked him for his failure to complete the tomb of Pope Julius, accused him of bad faith, and finally called for the destruction of the fresco. We have no evidence that Michelangelo actually received this letter, but Michelangelo did know of it because Aretino published it.

From that point on, the critics gathered around to join their voices to Aretino's. Perhaps as a literary device, or perhaps in response to the new political climate of the Catholic Reformation, Aretino took on the persona of one who was concerned about the simple folk and about what they might think of such a pornographic work being painted on the wall above the high altar in the Sistine Chapel. This is a far cry from his first letter in which he seemed to indicate a special knowledge and understanding of the subtleties of Michelangelo's work and placed himself among the literary elite. When he realized that there was a new audience for Michelangelo's fresco, an audience who would never see the work in its context but would only see it as a miniature reproduction thanks to the printing press, he realized also that all of Michelangelo's subtleties, all of his covert messages, both astronomical and reformist, would be lost to this audience. All the wider audience would see was the nudity.

In the end, Aretino failed to achieve his two goals: to destroy Michelangelo's reputation and perhaps to have the work destroyed. If he had achieved these, it would have been an act of real power, the power to sway public opinion. However, this was still the late Renaissance and not the age of television, and the decision regarding the destruction of the fresco remained in the hands of the pope and his court. What he did achieve, however, was an establishment of a tradition of criticism of the *Last Judgment*.

In 1564, Giovanni Andrea Gilio, a noted theologian added his voice to the critics. In his dialogue "On the Errors of Painting," he echoes Aretino by accusing Michelangelo of valuing art more than religion. Reggio, a character in his dialogue, says that Michelangelo was like a worried lover who thought that everything was acceptable to please his true love, art. However, he found it impossible to believe that "the secrets of nature or art are hidden in the genitalia, so that if an artist kept these covered he would be thought ignorant and clumsy."[9] Gilio also objected to Michelangelo's depiction of martyrs without their wounds. "Martyrs should have the scars of their wounds shining and resplendent, as a greater sign of their faith and constancy and of the cruelty of tyrants."[10] The fact that Michelangelo had left out the wounds of martyrs smelled like Lutheranism to the Counter-Reformation critics, because the Lutherans preferred to picture Christ resurrected, in glory—not on the cross, as the Spanish preferred to do, with a great display of gore. Gilio's criticism demonstrated that even the theological elite had changed. The Catholic Reformation had brought about a new evaluation of the relationship of the clergy with the people. It was no longer sufficient for the hierarchy to be well educated and to be artistically sophisticated. With the Protestant Reformation fully underway, the clergy recognized its need to minister to and to concern itself with the care of the faithful, lest they abandon the church for the new religions.

By this time, the Council of Trent had been in session for eighteen years, starting in 1545 and ending the year before Michelangelo's death in 1564. The censorship of the *Last Judgment* was well on its way when Gilio's dialogue was published in 1567. The Council was originally called into session by Pope Paul III, who had commissioned the *Last Judgment* and would have resisted any attempt to censor it. But he died in 1549, four years after the council had convened, and as Pope Clement had always known, Councils of Bishops chart their own course and produce their own results, often against the expressed wishes of the pope who convened them. By the time, therefore, that the Council had ruled on the *Last Judgment,* both Paul III and Julius III, popes who had been Michelangelo's most ardent supporters and defenders, were dead. Luckily for Michelangelo and the *Last Judgment,* Paul's immediate successor was Pope Julius III, who admired Michelangelo's work and defended him as vigorously as Pope Paul had done.

Julius died in 1555 and his successor Marcellus II died after one month in office. Cardinal Carafa, no friend of Michelangelo's and no lover of his *Last Judgment* fresco, was elected pope that same year and took the name Paul IV. He had first seen the fresco when he was a cardinal, and he suggested that the whole thing be painted over. Paul III would not hear of it, however, and instead had used Carafa to help lead the commission on internal church reform.

Within a short time after ascending the papal throne, Pope Paul IV began strengthening the Roman Inquisition, and from that point on, no one could consider himself immune from prosecution. Even cardinals found themselves in prison. Pope Paul did follow one tradition of the Renaissance, however. As soon as he was elected, he began to appoint members of his family to high positions within the church. The problem with Paul IV wasn't simply that he was a tyrant, but that he was a tyrant who believed that his will was the will of God. In a dangerous time, this made him especially dangerous.

This was a time of reaction both for Catholics and the Protestants. In Germany, the Lutheran church was growing more reactionary by the day, as was the Calvinist Church in Geneva. Largely, this was a result of the growing hostility between the various factions—Catholic to Protestant, Protestant to Protestant. Pope Paul IV was one more example of this intensified hostility and reactionary retreat.

Right away, in 1555, Paul issued a canon, or a papal law, creating the first Roman ghetto. Up until then, Rome had been a refuge for Jews, especially those fleeing the Spanish Inquisition—the more liberal papacy of the Renaissance had offered them a haven. With this single papal law, Jews were forced to live separate from the city, were locked in at night, and males were forced to wear yellow hats, women, yellow shawls. He promulgated this law because he believed that outside the Catholic Church there was no salvation. This pope wanted to separate the Jews from the rest of the Christian community in order to keep that community from being polluted by their "heresy." He also very quickly began to crack down on the remaining members of the Spirituali, immediately instigating an investigation of Bernardino Ochino and casting doubt on the orthodoxy of Cardinal Contarini. Pope Paul IV introduced the Index of Prohibited Books into Venice, then an independent trading state, because he suspected the Venetian printing trade of promoting Protestantism. All books written by Protestants were condemned, as were all translations of the Bible into Italian or German. His papacy picked up the reins of reform and drove church policies rapidly away from the Renaissance.

During his papacy, Paul also wanted to resolve the debate over Michelangelo's offending fresco. While he desired to have Michelangelo work for him as an architect on St. Peter's and as a designer of fortifications, the pope let it be known that he wanted Michelangelo to fix the *Last Judgment.* When he heard this, Michelangelo sent a reply back to the pope, heavy with sarcasm, telling Paul IV that pictures could easily be fixed, and that the pope should concentrate on fixing the world rather than art.

In December 1561, the Council of Trent decided to issue pronouncements about religious art. In its final decrees, the church council defined a very specific role for religious art, stating that Catholic churches should not use art for its own sake but for the sake of the instruction of the faithful. This was not a ban on religious art, because the council admitted the value of art as a welcome support to religious teaching. Essentially, the council was returning to the medieval position that art be used to instruct the faithful as a kind of visual catechism. Like the Theatines, the council was deeply concerned about the effect of unbridled religious art on the uneducated masses who depended upon the church for instruction and guidance.

Ten of the Council of Trent's final seventeen decrees in 1563 dealt with censorship. The decrees were promulgated one week before Michelangelo's death. The Council demanded that religious art portray the stories and mysteries of the faith, and that such art be used to remind the people of those stories and to further encourage them along the path toward salvation. For this purpose, the council required that religious art be clear, simple, and intelligible. They demanded that it abandon all attempts at subtlety and provide people with a realistic interpretation, that is, a truth that is unveiled and obvious to the people, that it be accurate, and that it follow proper decorum. By this they did not mean artistic decorum as Michelangelo did, but decorum as in the emerging moralistic definition that would ban even theologically correct depictions of the Last Judgment if the figures in the fresco were not properly clothed and if the person of Christ and of the apostles did not follow the expected format. In other words, they wanted the church to return to traditional depictions of the sacred mysteries. The council also specified that religious art had to provide an emotional stimulus to increase piety, that it should appeal to the emotions of the people in the pew, and that it support or even transcend the spoken word. Art was therefore to become a kind of sermon, or a visual aid for sermons.

As for Michelangelo's work, the council specifically required that adjustments be made to his *Last Judgment.* This meant reducing the amount of nudity in the fresco by painting over the offending parts. The fact that Michelangelo's fresco was the subject of a session in the Council of Trent says something about the shifting culture of the Counter-Reformation and the increasingly important role of doctrine in religious art. The damage to the fresco's reputation had been done, however, so that for centuries critics praised Michelangelo's ceiling fresco to heaven and denigrated the *Last Judgment* as a lesser work by an aging and exhausted man. Even John Addington Symonds, one of Michelangelo's greatest nineteenth-century biographers, criticized the *Last Judgment* as a lesser work.[11]

The pieces were all in place. Following the rules decreed by the Council of Trent, the reactionary Pope Pius IV hired one of Michelangelo's students, Daniele da Volterra, to make the "corrections" to the fresco, which earned him the nickname *Il Braghettone,* or the breeches-maker, using tempera to paint loincloths over the genitalia. Da Volterra also totally repainted Saint Blaise and nearly all of Saint Catherine, the two figures that had fueled the controversy over the fresco. For these areas, he had to remove the original *intonaco* and re-fresco the figures, retaining only Catherine's head, arms, and wheel from Michelangelo's original.

CHAPTER THIRTEEN

The Last Days of
Michelangelo Buonarroti

*A*lmost as soon as the *Last Judgment* was unveiled, Pope Paul III commissioned Michelangelo to paint two frescos in the new Pauline Chapel, his personal chapel adjoining the Sistine in the Vatican. This was a much smaller space because it was intended for the pope's private use although it also functioned as the room in which the cardinals elected the pope, in which the daily masses were sung, where ceremonies during the week preceding Easter took place, as well as several other religious functions in the papal calendar. Public entry was not allowed. It was the place that the pope usually said mass, attending ceremonies in the Sistine Chapel only a few times a year.

The first of these frescos painted by Michelangelo beginning in 1542 was the *Conversion of Paul,* which shows the saint lying in the road to Damascus, having just been struck from his horse. A crowd of angels and saints are flying overhead—most with clothes on—and Jesus is among them, flying upside-down with one hand outstretched and a beam of light passing between him and the blinded saint. Two groups of people on the ground surround Paul. To the right, some cower in fear or bewilderment, and some look up to the heavens. It's not certain whether they can see Jesus and the angels, but many seem awestruck as if they know they had encountered something uncanny. Just to the left of Paul is a Roman soldier in a tunic and leather doublet, carrying a round shield on his back. He stares up at the heavens while hoisting the shield up to protect himself. A standing figure behind Paul looks to the sky but in the wrong direction, as if he has heard something but doesn't know where it came from.

The general effect of this fresco is to tell the story of Paul's conversion within a powerful emotional context. Here, Michelangelo has returned to the kind of fresco that he painted on the Sistine ceiling. Gone are the crowds of nudes, even Jesus and the saints are wearing clothes, which leads one to conclude that the *Last Judgment* employed nudity for a very specific aesthetic purpose.

The second fresco is the *Crucifixion of Peter,* painted between 1546 and 1550. It was during this time, on February 25, 1547, that Michelangelo's dear friend Vittoria Colonna died. She had left Rome in 1541 when her brother Ascanio Colonna led a revolt against Pope Paul III. She moved back and forth between Orvieto and Viterbo for the next few years, but kept up a correspondence with Michelangelo. Her relationship with the painter didn't change when her family went to war with Michelangelo's patron, and when she eventually returned to Rome, she took up residence at the convent of San Silvestro, near his house. The two of them conversed regularly until her death.

The *Crucifixion of Peter* is the high point in Michelangelo's attempts to involve the audience in the drama of his frescos. Peter in a loincloth has been nailed to an inverted cross, and typical of Michelangelo, he painted no blood in the scene and showed no agony of terror on Peter's face. All around him is a standard crucifixion scene, with people milling around in little groups watching the crucifixion and a few Roman soldiers standing nearby to keep the crowds back. The hills in the background are barren, as if the land itself is empty. Clouds are forming in the sky, and the day is growing dark. In the middle of all this, Peter is not looking at his tormentors or at the crowds but has turned his head around so that he looks directly into the eyes of the spectator. Since the spectator was almost certainly the pope and the conclave of cardinals, they must thus confront every day the eyes of the first pope staring at them at the moment of his martyrdom, involving every pope and cardinal who would see it, reminding them of their responsibilities, and compelling them to respond in some ways to his glance.

These two frescos were much smaller than anything Michelangelo had ever done before, about 20 feet by 21 feet, but at the end of the painting, Michelangelo was exhausted. Because of his age and failing health, these two frescos took longer to paint than the Sistine ceiling. Still, they were painted with the same passion and power of the earlier frescos. His colors are even brighter and his figures are more massive than before. By this time, Michelangelo's work had influenced a style of art called Mannerism that soon spread over Europe, culminating in the late sixteenth century with its last great practitioner, El Greco. The *Conversion of Paul* and the *Crucifixion of Peter* are early examples of the Mannerist style. The way he has posed the characters, crisscrossing their arms and legs, expressing emotion in their faces, and the way he created a crowd of bodies in a seemingly boundless space were typical of the style.

Michelangelo was well into his 70s when he finished the frescos in the Pauline Chapel. In 1547, the year Vittoria Colonna died, Pope Paul III had named him chief architect for the building of St. Peter's and also sent him to work on the new Farnese Palace. He accepted these commissions reluctantly because he could feel that age was finally catching up with him. A kidney stone troubled him, making urination difficult. Michelangelo's letters constantly complained of his age and feebleness.[1] He played with the idea of going on a pilgrimage to the shrine of Santiago de Compostela in Spain, one of the premier pilgrimage sites in Europe. His health continued to decline, however, and he wrote a letter in the spring of 1547 to his friend Benedetto Varchi in which he complained that "not only am I old, but I am almost among the number of the dead." Michelangelo's spirituality had become the most important thing in his life. In a poem he wrote in 1553, he said:

> Once, my heart burned even dunked in ice
> But that burning fire is like ice to me, Love
> Now that the unbreakable knot has been untied
> And what was once a happy feast has become death to me.[2]

Despite what Gilio would later write, Michelangelo's spirituality and not his art was the dominating force behind the *Last Judgment*. Savonarola's long dead voice still spoke to him, crying out for reform. Dante's poetry guided him. But most of all, his own yearning for salvation pushed him forward, to create a fresco that would daunt and terrify viewers for centuries. Perhaps, as Michelangelo had hoped, some would be converted by it.

Pope Paul III died in 1549, before Michelangelo had finished the *Crucifixion* fresco but he did see the completed *Conversion* fresco. His successor, Julius III, continued to employ Michelangelo as the chief architect for St. Peter's.

During this time, a controversy broke out between Michelangelo and a cabal of opponents, a group that Giorgio Vasari called the "Sangallo sect" who resented the fact that the reconstruction of St. Peter's was given over to Michelangelo after Antonio da Sangallo, the previous architect, died. This group, led by Nanni di Baccio Bigio, wanted to take over the commission themselves. They believed that Michelangelo was a usurper and that the commission should have been theirs. Michelangelo didn't help matters much by ordering changes in Sangallo's design, abandoning his original plan for a church with a long nave in order to return to a more centrally planned monument. When he received opposition to his new plan, Michelangelo fired off a sarcastic letter to the Prefect of the Deputies of the Fabric of St. Peter's, laying out all of his objections to Sangallo's plan. In the end, they followed Michelangelo's design, including his design for the great dome.

On March 23, 1555, Julius died, leaving the church in the feeble hands of Marcellus II, who died three weeks later, to be succeeded by Pope Paul IV whose anti-Spanish policy led to a war against Spain. The Duke of Alba sent an army to lay siege to Rome, and Michelangelo, fearing another sack, went on pilgrimage to Loretto. Nothing came of the threatened attack, however, and Michelangelo got only as far as Spoleto before a rider caught up with him with orders for him to return to work on St. Peter's. When Paul IV finally died in August 1559, an angry crowd took his statue, broke it into pieces and threw it into the Tiber. His successor was Pope Pius IV, who ordered the censorship of the *Last Judgment* in response to the decree from the Council of Trent.

During those years, Michelangelo continued to work on St. Peter's, but the work became more difficult as he aged. In November 1555 he learned that his brother Gismondo had died in Florence, and at this same time his beloved assistant Urbino lay dying in Michelangelo's house. He had known the man for 25 years and had loved him like a son. When Urbino died, Michelangelo grieved deeply and fell into a depression. On January 4, 1556, in a letter he wrote to his nephew Lionardo, he said:

> I must tell you that last night, the third day of December at
> 9 o'clock, Francesco, called Urbino, passed from this life to my
> intense grief, leaving me so stricken and troubled that it would have
> been easier to die with him, because of the love I bore him, which

merited no less; for he was a fine man, full of loyalty and devotion; so that owing to his death I now seem to be lifeless myself and can find no peace.[3]

Michelangelo took over the support of Urbino's widow and children, even after she remarried. On February 14, 1564, Michelangelo suffered a stroke. His friend Tiberio Calcagni, a young Florentine sculptor who had taken Urbino's place, found him wandering outside in the rain. Calcagni spoke to him, saying that he shouldn't be outside in bad weather. Michelangelo said, "What do you want me to do? I am ill and I cannot find peace anywhere."[4] Calcagni wrote to Michelangelo's nephew Lionardo, saying that he was most certainly dying. The next day, Michelangelo tried to write a letter to Lionardo but was unable to and so he asked Daniele da Volterra to write the letter for him asking Lionardo to come to Rome. The weather in Italy at that time of year had been dismal, and the roads were muddy up and down the peninsula. While they waited for Lionardo, Tommaso de Cavalieri and Daniele da Volterra never left his side. On February 18, 1564, in the presence of Tomasso de Cavalieri, Michelangelo died "about the time of the Ave Maria."

Soon after Michelangelo died, a debate broke out about where to bury his body. At first, his body was carried to the Roman Church of Sant' Apostoli. There was also a plan to bury him in St. Peter's, until Lionardo arrived in Rome on February 21 and began to make arrangements to take his uncle's body to Florence, telling everyone that Michelangelo had desired to be buried in his native city. But the Roman people didn't want to let him go, and so Lionardo smuggled his uncle's coffin, disguised as a bale of wool, out of the city. Days later, on March 10, Michelangelo's body arrived in Florence. Vasari had accompanied the body and the coffin, and signed them in at the customs house. He had been the agent of the Florentine Academy of

Drawing, which planned to organize a citywide memorial service at the church of San Lorenzo. They moved the body from the customs house to the Compagnia Dell Assunta. The following evening, the entire Academy of Art accompanied Michelangelo's body in a torch-light procession to his old parish church of Santa Croce.

A large crowd had gathered around the body and the order came down to open the casket so that all could see Michelangelo in death. They sent for a representative from the customs house to come and break open the seals. When they did so, they were amazed to find that his body had not deteriorated and that he looked as if he had just died. Don Vincenzo Borghini, the prior of the Foundling Hospital and the president of the academy announced to all that it was a sign of God's favor that Michelangelo's body had been preserved from decay.[5] This is the kind of story that often circulated after the deaths of saints. With much ceremony, the Florentine academy lay Michelangelo's body to rest in the Church of Santa Croce. The *Last Judgment* fresco remained a source of controversy, and while there were several attempts to tame its nudity with strategically placed loincloths and tunics, the fresco endured, gathering dirt over the centuries.

There were several attempts to clean it over the years; some did more harm than good. On April 8, 1998, Pope John Paul II celebrated mass in the Chapel to reveal the most complete restoration of the fresco ever done, where art and science collaborated to bring the great fresco back to life. If you had visited the Chapel before the restoration, you would hardly know the fresco was there. Now, however, those who see it are amazed by it, and no one ever forgets the moment they saw the Day of Judgment.

FURTHER READING

Barnes, Bernadine. *Michelangelo's Last Judgment: The Renaissance Response*. Berkeley, CA: University of California Press, 1998.

Blech, Benjamin and Roy Doliner. *The Sistine Secrets: Michelangelo's Forbidden Messages in the Heart of the Vatican*. New York, NY: Harper One, 2008.

Bull, George. *Michelangelo: A Biography*. New York, NY: St. Martin's Griffin, 1995.

Buonarroti, Michelangelo. *Rime*. Introduzione di Giovanni Testori. Milano, Italia: Biblioteca Universale Rizzoli, 1975, 1988.

Chapman, Hugo. *Michelangelo Drawings: Closer to the Master*. New Haven, CT: Yale University Press, 2005.

Clements, Robert J. *Michelangelo's Theory of Art*. New York, NY: Gramercy Publishing Company, 1961.

Condivi, Ascanio. *The Life of Michelangelo*. Translated by Alice Sedgwick Wohl, second edition. University Park, PA: Pennsylvania State University Press, 2001. First published by Louisiana University Press, 1976.

Coughlan, Robert. *The World of Michelangelo: 1475–1564*, 2 vols. New York, NY: Time-Life Books, 1966.

De Hollanda, Francisco. *Four Dialogues on Painting*. Translated by Aubrey F. G. Bell. London, UK: Oxford University Press, 1928. Hyperion reprint edition 1980, 1993.

De Tolnay, Charles. *Michelangelo, the Final Period: Last Judgment, Frescos of the Pauline Chapel, Last Pietas* . Princeton, NJ: Princeton University Press, 1960, 1971.

De Vecchi, Pierluigi. *Michelangelo: The Vatican Frescos with an essay on the restoration by Gianluigi Colalucci*. New York: Abbeville Press Publishers, 1996.

Guicciardini, Francesco. *Dialogue on the Government of Florence*. Edited and translated by Alison Brown. Cambridge, UK: Cambridge University Press, 1994.

———. *The History of Italy*, translated, edited, with notes and an introduction by Sidney Alexander. Princeton, NJ: Princeton University Press, 1969.

Guicciardini, Luigi. *The Sack of Rome*. Translated with an Introduction and Notes by James H. McGregor. New York: Italica Press, 1993.

Hall, James. *Michelangelo and the Reinvention of the Human Body*. New York, NY: Farrar, Straus and Giroux, 2005.

Hibbard, Howard. *Michelangelo*, second edition. Boulder, CO: Westview Press, 1974.

Hughes, Anthony. *Michelangelo*. London: Phaidon Press Limited, 1997.

Hutton, Edward. *Pietro Aretino: The Scourge of Princes.* Boston, MA: Houghton Mifflin Company, 1922.

Jardine, Lisa. *Worldly Goods: A New History of the Renaissance.* New York: W.W. Norton & Company, 1996.

Johnson, Paul. *A History of Christianity.* New York, NY: Simon and Schuster/ Touchstone Book, 1976.

King, Ross. *Michelangelo and the Pope's Ceiling.* New York: Penguin Books, 2003.

Martines, Lauro. *Fire in the City: Savonarola and the Struggle for the Soul of Renaissance Florence.* New York, NY: Oxford University Press, 2006.

McCornick, W. *Michelangelo: The Works – The Sistine Chapel.* Roma: Casa Editrice Lozzi, 1971.

Michelangelo the Last Judgment: A Glorious Restoration. General editor, Sandro Chierici. New York, NY: Henry Abrams, Inc., 1997.

Michelangelo: Selected Readings. Edited with an introduction by William E. Wallace. New York, NY: Garland Publishing, Inc., 1999.

Merrifield, Mary P. *The Art of Fresco Painting in the Middle Ages and the Renaissance.* Mineola, NY: Dover Publications, Inc., 2003. Originally published: *The Art of Fresco Painting as Practiced by the Old Italian and Spanish Masters , with a Preliminary Inquiry into the Nature of the Colours Used in Fresco Painting, with Observations and Notes,* originally published by Charles Gilpin and Arthur Wallis. London: C. Gilpin, 1846.

Murray, Linda. *Michelangelo.* London: Thames and Hudson Ltd., 1980. New York, NY: Thames and Hudson, 1985.

Nickerson, Angela K. *A Journey into Michelangelo's Rome.* Berkeley, CA: Roaring Forties Press, 2008.

Paolucci, Antonio; Monica Bietti and Francesca Fiorelli Malesi. *Sacred Florence: Art and Architecture.* Translated by Huw Evans. New York, NY: Barnes and Noble Publishing, 2006.

Ramsden, E.H. *The Letters of Michelangelo.* Translated from the original Tuscan, edited and annotated in Two Volumes. Stanford, CA: Stanford University Press, 1963.

Rabb, Theodore K. *The Last Days of the Renaissance and the March to Modernity.* New York, NY: Basic Books, 2006.

Rolland, Romain. *Michelangelo.* Translated by Frederick Street. New York, NY: Albert and Charles Boni, Inc., 1935.

Sala, Charles. *Michelangelo: Sculptor, Painter, Architect.* Paris: Editions Pierre Terrail, 2003.

Saslow, James M. *The Poetry of Michelangelo: An Annotated Translation.* New Haven, CT: Yale University Press, 1991.

Scigliano, Eric. *Michelangelo's Mountain: The Quest for Perfection in the Marble Quarries of Carrara.* New York: Free Press, 2005.

Stemp, Richard. *The Secret Language of the Renaissance: Decoding the Hidden Symbolism of Italian Art.* London: Duncan Baird Publishers, 2006.

Symonds, John Addington. *The Life of Michelangelo Buonarroti.* Charleston, SC: BiblioBazaar, 2006.

Vasari, Giorgio. *The Lives of the Artists: A New Translation by Julia Conaway Bondanella and Peter Bondanella*. Oxford, UK: Oxford University Press, 1991.

————. *On Technique: Being the Introduction to the Three Arts of Design, Architecture, Sculpture and Painting, Prefixed to the Lives of the Most Excellent Painters, Sculptors and Architects*. Mineola, NY: Dover Publications, Inc., 1960. An unabridged and unaltered republication of the work first published by J. M. Dent & Company in 1907, except that the frontispiece and Plate XII, which appeared in color in the original edition, are here reproduced in black and white.

Vatican Museums, The. *The Last Judgment: Vol. I. The Restoration; Vol. II. The Plates*. Preface by Francesco Buranelli, General Manager of Pontifical Monuments, Museums and Galleries. New York, NY: Rizzoli International Publications, Inc., 1999.

Von Pastor, Dr. Ludwig. *History of the Popes from the Close of the Middle Ages*, drawn from the secret archives of the Vatican and other original sources. Vol. I; Vol. V ed. by Frederick Ignatius Antrobus. London: Kegan Paul, Trench, Trubner and Co., Ltd., 1938. Vol. XII, (1534-1549); Vol. XVI, Pius IV (1559–1565); Vol. XVIII, Pius V (1566–1572); Vol. XIX, Gregory XIII (1572–1585); Vol. XX, Gregory XIII (1572–1585). ed. Ralph Kerr. London: Routledge and Kegan Paul Ltd. St. Louis, MO: B. Herder Book Co., first published in England in 1930, reprinted in 1952.

Wadley, Nicholas. *Michelangelo*. London: Hamlyn Publishing Group Limited, 1965.

NOTES

INTRODUCTION

1. Girolamo Savonarola, *Il Quaresimale del 1491: La certezza profetica di un mondo nuovo*, eds, Armando F. Verde and Elettra Giaconi, nos. 300, 302. (Florence: Sismel, 2001).
2. The term "usury" has undergone a number of changes over the centuries. Throughout the Middle Ages and the Renaissance, the Catholic Church condemned all lending money for interest. Scholastic theology taught that lending for interest was a variation of theft, double charging the borrower, charging for both the thing and for the use of the thing. Thomas Aquinas claimed that it would be immoral to charge a man for a bottle of wine, and then charge him once again for drinking it.
3. Arthur Vermeersch. "Usury," *The Catholic Encyclopedia*. Vol. 15. (New York: Robert Appleton Company, 1912), http://www.newadvent.org/cathen/15235c.htm (accessed December 8, 2008).
4. Lauro Martinez, *Fire in the City: Savonarola and the Struggle for the Soul of Renaissance Florence* (Oxford: Oxford University Press, 2006), p. 71.
5. Alexander VI had at least eight children, of whom five are well known. His first mistress, Vannozza dei Cattani bore him four children, Giovanni (b. 1474), later duke of Gandia, Cesare (b. 1476), Lucrezia (b. 1480), and Goffredo, (b. 1481, or 1482). His next mistress was Giulia Farnese, the sister of Alessandro Farnese, who would become Pope Paul III. Giula, also called Giulia Bella, or Beautiful Giulia, bore him a daughter, Laura.
6. There are eight officially recognized bad popes:
   Stephen VI (896–897), who had his predecessor exhumed, tried, de-fingered, briefly reburied, and then thrown in the Tiber River; John XII (955–964), who gave land to a mistress, murdered several people, and was killed by a man who caught him in bed with his wife; Benedict IX (1032–1044,1045,1047–1048), who sold the papacy; Boniface VIII (1294–1303), whom Dante lampooned in the *Divine Comedy;* Urban VI (1378–1389), who complained that he did not hear enough screaming when his enemies were tortured; Alexander VI (1492–1503), a Borgia, the father of Cesare and Lucrezia, who tried to give the papacy to his illegitimate children and had Savonarola executed; Leo X (1513–1521), the party animal of the Medici family who once spent one seventh of the Vatican reserve fund on a single ceremony; Clement VII (1523–1534), also a Medici, whose poor diplomatic judgment with France, Spain, and Germany got Rome sacked.

7. Lauro Martinez, *Fire in the City: Savonarola and the Struggle for the Soul of Renaissance Florence* (Oxford: Oxford University Press, 2006), p. 124.

8. Pasquale Villari, *Life and Times of Girolamo Savonarola*, trans. Linda Villari, Eleventh ed. (New York: Scribner's, 1918), p. 126.

9. Pasquale Villari, *Life and Times of Girolamo Savonarola*, trans. Linda Villari, Eleventh ed. (New York: Scribner's, 1918), p. 126.

10. Pasquale Villari, *Life and Times of Girolamo Savonarola*, trans. Linda Villari, Eleventh ed. (New York: Scribner's, 1918), p. 147.

11. Pasquale Villari, *Life and Times of Girolamo Savonarola*, trans. Linda Villari, Eleventh ed. (New York: Scribner's, 1918), pp. 147–148.

12. Savonarola, Girolamo, *Prediche sopra aggeo e con il trattata circa il regimento e governo della citta di Firenze*, Ed., L. Firpi, nos. 321, 326, 327, 329 (Rome: Belardetti, 1965). See also Pasquale Villari, *Life and Times of Girolamo Savonarola*, trans. Linda Villari, Eleventh ed. (New York: Scribner's, 1918), p. 158.

13. Pasquale Villari, *Life and Times of Girolamo Savonarola*, trans. Linda Villari, Eleventh ed. (New York: Scribner's, 1918), p. 608.

14. Benvenuto Cellini, *Autobiography of Benvenuto Cellini*, trans. John Addington Symonds, Harvard Classics, V. 31, New York: P.F. Collier and Sons, 1910, p. 72.

15. Francesco Guicciardini, *The History of Italy*, trans. Sidney Alexander (Princeton: Princeton University Press, 1969), p. 389.

16. Benvenuto Cellini, *Autobiography of Benvenuto Cellini*, trans. John Addington Symonds, Harvard Classics, V. 31 (New York: P.F. Collier and Sons, 1910), p. 155.

CHAPTER ONE

1. Ascanio Condivi, *Vita di Michelangelo Buonarroti*, con saggi di M. Hirst e C. Elam (Firenze: Studio per edizione scelte, 1998), p.18.

2. Michelangelo Buonarroti, *Il carteggio di Michelangelo*, edizione postuma di Giovanni Poggi, a cura di Paola Barocchi e Renzo Ristori (Firenze: Sansoni, 1965), Vol. III, DCXXVIII.

3. Michelangelo Buonarroti, *Il carteggio di Michelangelo*, edizione postuma di Giovanni Poggi, a cura di Paola Barocchi e Renzo Ristori (Firenze: Sansoni, 1965), Vol. III, DCCXXVII.

4. George Bull, *Michelangelo: A Biography* (New York: St. Martin's Griffin, 1995), p. 270.

5. Michelangelo Buonarroti, *The Letters of Michelangelo*, vol. I, trans. E.H. Ramsden (Stanford, CA: Stanford University Press, 1963), letter 125, p. 114.

6. Michelangelo Buonarroti, *Il carteggio di Michelangelo*, edizione postuma di Giovanni Poggi, a cura di Paola Barocchi e Renzo Ristori (Firenze: Sansoni, 1965), Vol. III, DCCXXX.

7. Michelangelo Buonarroti, *Il carteggio di Michelangelo,* edizione postuma di Giovanni Poggi, a cura di Paola Barocchi e Renzo Ristori (Firenze: Sansoni, 1965), Vol. III, CMXXXII.

8. Michelangelo Buonarroti, *Il carteggio di Michelangelo,* edizione postuma di Giovanni Poggi, a cura di Paola Barocchi e Renzo Ristori (Firenze: Sansoni, 1965), Vol. III, CMXVI.

9. Michelangelo Buonarroti, *Il carteggio di Michelangelo,* edizione postuma di Giovanni Poggi, a cura di Paola Barocchi e Renzo Ristori (Firenze: Sansoni, 1965), Vol, III, CMXXXII.

10. Michelangelo, *Rime,* introduzione di Giovanni Testori, cronologia, promessa e note a cura di Ettore Barelli (Milano: Biblioteca Universale Rizzoli, 1975), no. 71, p. 127.

11. Michelangelo, *Rime,* introduzione di Giovanni Testori, cronologia, promessa e note a cura di Ettore Barelli (Milano: Biblioteca Universale Rizzoli, 1975), no. 66, p. 115.

12. Michelangelo Buonarroti, *Il carteggio di Michelangelo,* edizione postuma di Giovanni Poggi, a cura di Paola Barocchi e Renzo Ristori (Firenze: Sansoni, 1965), Vol. IV, CMXV.

13. Michelangelo Buonarroti, *Il carteggio di Michelangelo,* edizione postuma di Giovanni Poggi, a cura di Paola Barocchi e Renzo Ristori (Firenze: Sansoni, 1965), Vol. IV, CMXXI.

14. Michelangelo, *Rime,* introduzione di Giovanni Testori, cronologia, promessa e note a cura di Ettore Barelli (Milano: Biblioteca Universale Rizzoli, 1975), p. 138.

15. Michelangelo, *Rime,* introduzione di Giovanni Testori, cronologia, promessa e note a cura di Ettore Barelli (Milano: Biblioteca Universale Rizzoli, 1975), no. 76, p. 131.

CHAPTER TWO

1. J. Rudnicki, *Nicholas Copernicus* (Mikolaj Kopernik), 1473–1543 (London, 1943), p. 56.

2. Latin text found in Valerie Shrimplin, *Sun Symbolism and Cosmology in Michelangelo's Last Judgment* (Kirksville: Truman State University Press, 2000), p. 282, n. 98.

3. Michelangelo Buonarroti, *Il carteggio di Michelangelo,* edizione postuma di Giovanni Poggi, a cura di Paola Barocchi e Renzo Ristori (Firenze: Sansoni,1965), Vol. IV, CMXII.

4. Francesco Guicciardini, *The History of Italy,* trans. and ed. Sidney Alexander (Princeton: Princeton University Press, 1969), p. 440.

5. Marsilio Ficino, *Theologia Platonica de Immortalitate Animae (Platonic Theology).* Latin with English translation (Cambridge: Harvard University Press, Six Volumes. 2001–2006).

6. Francesco Guicciardini, *The History of Italy,* trans. and ed. Sidney Alexander (Princeton: Princeton University Press, 1969), p. 442. Pope Clement was roundly hated by nearly everyone in Rome by the time he died. Guicciardini assesses his character as one of great capacity if "his timidity had not corrupted his power of judgment."

CHAPTER THREE

1. Charles Holroyd, *Michelangelo Buonarroti, with Translations of the Life of the Master by his Scholar, Ascanio Condivi, and Three Dialogues from the Portuguese by Francisco D'Ollanda* (London: Duckworth and Co., 1903), p. 66.
2. Ascanio Condivi, *Vita di Michelangelo Buonarroti,* con saggi di M. Hirst e C. Elam (Firenze: Studio per edizione scelte, 1998), pp. 43–44.
3. The Castel Sant'Angelo is a round fortress that sits next to the Tiber, and was traditionally part of the Vatican. It was once the Mausoleum of the Roman emperor Hadrian, but in the Middle Ages, it was rebuilt and fortified to be a refuge for popes during warfare.
4. Ascanio Condivi, *Vita di Michelangelo Buonarroti,* con saggi di M. Hirst e C. Elam (Firenze: Studio per edizione scelte, 1998), p. 34.
5. Ascanio Condivi, *Vita di Michelangelo Buonarroti,* con saggi di M. Hirst e C. Elam (Firenze: Studio per edizione scelte, 1998), p. 39.
6. Ascanio Condivi, *Vita di Michelangelo Buonarroti,* con saggi di M. Hirst e C. Elam (Firenze: Studio per edizione scelte, 1998), pp. 39–40.
7. Ascanio Condivi, *Vita di Michelangelo Buonarroti,* con saggi di M. Hirst e C. Elam (Firenze: Studio per edizione scelte, 1998), p. 42.
8. Ascanio Condivi, *Vita di Michelangelo Buonarroti,* con saggi di M. Hirst e C. Elam (Firenze: Studio per edizione scelte, 1998), p. 42.
9. Ascanio Condivi, *Vita di Michelangelo Buonarroti,* con saggi di M. Hirst e C. Elam (Firenze: Studio per edizione scelte, 1998), p. 42.
10. Ascanio Condivi, *Vita di Michelangelo Buonarroti,* con saggi di M. Hirst e C. Elam (Firenze: Studio per edizione scelte, 1998), p. 43.
11. Ascanio Condivi, *Vita di Michelangelo Buonarroti,* con saggi di M. Hirst e C. Elam (Firenze: Studio per edizione scelte, 1998), p. 43.
12. Ascanio Condivi, *Vita di Michelangelo Buonarroti,* con saggi di M. Hirst e C. Elam (Firenze: Studio per edizione scelte, 1998), p. 44.
13. Ascanio Condivi, *Vita di Michelangelo Buonarroti,* con saggi di M. Hirst e C. Elam (Firenze: Studio per edizione scelte, 1998), p. 44.
14. Ascanio Condivi, *Vita di Michelangelo Buonarroti,* con saggi di M. Hirst e C. Elam (Firenze: Studio per edizione scelte, 1998), p. 53.
15. Michelangelo Buonarroti, *Il carteggio di Michelangelo,* edizione postuma di Giovanni Poggi, a cura di Paola Barocchi e Renzo Ristori (Firenze : Sansoni, 1965), Vol. 1, CXXVII.
16. Michelangelo, *The Letters of Michelangelo,* vol. 1, trans. E.H. Ramsden (Stanford: Stanford University Press, 1963), p. 252.

17. Michelangelo, *The Letters of Michelangelo*, vol. 1, trans. E.H. Ramsden (Stanford: Stanford University Press, 1963), p. 256.
18. Michelangelo, *The Letters of Michelangelo*, vol. 1, trans. E.H. Ramsden (Stanford: Stanford University Press, 1963), p. 257.
19. Michelangelo, *The Letters of Michelangelo*, vol. 1, trans. E.H. Ramsden (Stanford: Stanford University Press, 1963), p. 258.
20. Michelangelo Buonarroti, *Il carteggio di Michelangelo*, edizione postuma di Giovanni Poggi, a cura di Paola Barocchi e Renzo Ristori (Firenze: Sansoni, 1965), Vol. IV, DCCCXXIV.
21. Ascanio Condivi, *Vita di Michelagnolo Buonarroti*, con saggi di M. Hirst e C. Elam (Firenze: Studio per edizione scelte, 1998), p. 65.
22. Ascanio Condivi, *Vita di Michelagnolo Buonarroti*, con saggi di M. Hirst e C. Elam (Firenze: Studio per edizione scelte, 1998), p. 66.
23. Ascanio Condivi, *Vita di Michelagnolo Buonarroti*, con saggi di M. Hirst e C. Elam (Firenze: Studio per edizione scelte, 1998), p. 66.
24. The scudo had replaced the florin during the reign of Pope Paul III. The scudo was the official currency of the papal states until 1866, when it was replaced by the lira, equal to the Italian lira. The coin was made from silver, with a shield (*scutum* in Latin) stamped onto the surface. It was divided into 100 baiocchi (sing. baiocco), each of 5 quattrini.
25. Michelangelo Buonarroti, *Il carteggio di Michelangelo*, edizione postuma di Giovanni Poggi, a cura di Paola Barocchi e Renzo Ristori (Firenze: Sansoni, 1965), Vol. IV, CMVIII.
26. Francesco Guicciardini, *The History of Italy*, trans. Sidney Alexander (Princeton: Princeton University Press), p. 19.

CHAPTER FOUR

1. Helmut Wohl, Introduction, *Ascanio Condivi, Life of Michelangelo*, trans. Alice Sedgwick Wohl, ed. Helmut Wohl, Second Edition (University Park: Pennsylvania State University Press, 1976), p. xiii.
2. Ascanio Condivi, *Vita di Michelagnolo Buonarroti*, con saggi di M. Hirst e C. Elam (Firenze: Studio per edizione scelte, 1998), p. 74.
3. "Sebastiano Veniziano," Giorgio Vasari, *Le Vite de Piu Eccellente Pittori, Scultori e Architettori, Testo a cura di Rosama Bettarini, Commento Secolare a cura di Paola Barocchi*, Vol. III (Firenze: Studio per Edizioni Scelte, 1966), p. 102.
4. Michelangelo, *Rime*, introduzione di Giovanni Testori, cronologia, promessa e note a cura di Ettore Barelli (Milano: Biblioteca Universale Rizzoli, 1975), no. 276, p. 314.
5. E.H. Ramsden, Introduction, *The Letters of Michelangelo*, trans. E.H. Ramsden, Vol. II (Stanford: Stanford University Press, 1963), p. xxi.
6. Michelangelo Buonarroti, *Il carteggio di Michelangelo*, edizione postuma di Giovanni Poggi, a cura di Paola Barocchi e Renzo Ristori, (Firenze: Sansoni, 1965), Vol. III, DCCLII.

7. Giorgio Vasari, *The Lives of the Artists,* trans. Julia Conaway Bondanella and Peter Bondanella (Oxford: Oxford University Press, 1998), p. 101.
8. Ross King, *Michelangelo and the Pope's Ceiling* (New York: Penguin, 2003), pp. 104–105.
9. Valerie Shrimplin, *Sun Symbolism and Cosmology in Michelangelo's Last Judgment* (Kirksville: Truman State University Press, 2000), p. 270.
10. Giorgio Vasari, *On Technique,* trans. Louisa S. Maclehose (New York: Dover, 1960), p. 221.
11. Giorgio Vasari, *On Technique,* trans. Louisa S. Maclehose (New York: Dover, 1960), p. 221.

Chapter Five

1. Benjamin Blech and Roy Doliner, *The Sistine Secrets: Michelangelo's Forbidden Messages in the Heart of the Vatican* (San Francisco: Harper One, 2008). p. 6. The current chapel is a replica of the *heichal,* or the back part of Solomon's temple. The fact that this was forbidden in the Talmud didn't matter, at least not to Sixtus, the architect, even though creating a copy of Solomon's Temple was a taboo among Greek Christians for years.
2. George Bull, *Michelangelo: A Biography,* (New York: St. Martin Griffin, 1995), p. 389.
3. John 6: 68.
4. Giorgio Vasari, *The Lives of the Artists,* trans. Julia Conaway Bondanella and Peter Bondanella, (Oxford: Oxford University Press, 1998), p. 262.
5. "Pietro Perugino," *Giorgio Vasari, Le Vite de Piu Eccellente Pittori, Scultori e Architettori, nel redazioni del 1550 e 1568,* Vol. VI (Firenze: Studio per Edizioni Scelte, 1966), p. 608.
6. The original Latin text was taken from the Graduale Romano Seraphico, Ordinis Fratrum Minorum, typis Societatis S. Joannis Evangelistae, Desclee & Socii, Paris, 1932, in the sequence for the Missa pro Defunctis, pp. 97–100. Author's translation.
7. Charles de Tolnay, *Michelangelo: The Final Period,* Vol. 5 (Princeton, NJ: Princeton University Press, 1960), p. 30.
8. Ross King, *Michelangelo and the Pope's Ceiling* (New York: Penguin, 2003), p. 124.
9. Fabrizio Manizinelli, "The History, Execution Technique, First Censorship, and Restoration Interventions," *The Last Judgment,* Vol. I, The Restoration (New York: Rizzoli, 1999), p. 10.
10. Fabrizio Manizinelli, "The History, Execution Technique, First Censorship, and Restoration Interventions," *The Last Judgment,* Vol. I, The Restoration (New York: Rizzoli, 1999), p. 11.
11. Mary P. Merryfield, *The Art of Fresco Painting in the Middle Ages and the Renaissance* (New York: Dover, 2003), p. 7.

12. George Bull, *Michelangelo: A Biography,* (New York: St. Martin's Griffin, 1995), p. 389, pp. 270–272.
13. Pietro Aretino, *Lettere Scritte a Pietro Aretino, a cura di Paolo Procaccioli,* Vol. I (Roma: Salerno Editrice, 2003), XXXVIII.
14. Michelangelo Buonarroti, *Il carteggio di Michelangelo,* edizione postuma di Giovanni Poggi, a cura di Paola Barocchi e Renzo Ristori (Firenze: Sansoni, 1965), Vol. III, CMLV.

CHAPTER SIX

1. Muhammad Arshad and Michael Fitzgerald, *Journal of Medical Biography,* 2004, May 12 (2): 115–120.
2. Howard Hibbard, *Michelangelo,* Second Edition, (Boulder: Westview Press, 1974), p. 184.
3. *The Letters of Michelangelo,* trans. E.H. Ramsden, Vol. II, Letter 396 (Stanford: Stanford University Press, 1963), p. 150.
4. Michelangelo, *Rime,* introduzione di Giovanni Testori, cronologia, promessa e note a cura di Ettore Barelli (Milano: Biblioteca Universale Rizzoli, 1975), no. 267, p. 303.
5. John Addington Symonds, *The Life of Michelangelo Buonarroti,* (Bibliobazaar, 2006), p. 300.
6. Francis Schaefer, "Gasparo Contarini." *The Catholic Encyclopedia.* Vol. 4. (New York: Robert Appleton Company, 1908). Accessed Feb. 19, 2008 <http://www.newadvent.org/cathen/04323c.htm>.

CHAPTER SEVEN

1. Vittoria Colonna (Epistola a Ferrante Francesco d'Avalos, suo consorte, nella rotta di Ravenna). Luna Naples, October 1536, Bullock, *Rime,* 280), V:137–139. Author's translation.
2. Henry Roscoe, *Vittoria Colonna: Her Life and Poems,* (London: Macmillan, 1868), pp. 42–43.
3. Una Roman D'Elia, Drawing Christ's Blood: Michelangelo, Vittoria Colonna, and the Aesthetics of Reform, *Renaissance Quarterly,* Vol. 59, No. 1, Spring 2006, pp. 90–129.
4. Una Roman D'Elia, Drawing Christ's Blood: Michelangelo, Vittoria Colonna, and the Aesthetics of Reform, *Renaissance Quarterly,* Vol. 59, No. 1, Spring 2006, pp. 90–129.
5. Michelangelo, *Rime,* introduzione di Giovanni Testori, cronologia, promessa e note a cura di Ettore Barelli (Milano: Biblioteca Universale Rizzoli, 1975), 199, p. 328. Author's translation.

6. Francisco de Hollanda, *Four Dialogues on Painting,* trans. Aubrey F.G. Bell (Westport, CN.: Hyperion, 1928), p. xi.

7. Francisco de Hollanda, *Four Dialogues on Painting,* trans. Aubrey F.G. Bell (Westport, CN.: Hyperion, 1928).

8. Francisco de Hollanda, *Four Dialogues on Painting,* trans. Aubrey F.G. Bell (Westport, CN.: Hyperion, 1928), p. 7. Also, see *The Letters of Michelangelo,* trans. E.H. Ramsden, Vol. 2 (Stanford: Stanford University Press, 1963), p. xxii.

9. Francisco de Hollanda, *Four Dialogues on Painting,* trans. Aubrey F.G. Bell (Westport, CN.: Hyperion, 1928), p. 8.

10. Francisco de Hollanda, *Four Dialogues on Painting,* trans. Aubrey F.G. Bell (Westport, CN.: Hyperion, 1928), p. 9.

11. Michelangelo, *Letters of Michelangelo,* trans. E.H. Ramsden, Vol. 2 (Stanford: Stanford University Press, 1963), p. xxiii.

12. Francisco de Hollanda, *Four Dialogues on Painting,* trans. Aubrey F.G. Bell (Westport, CN.: Hyperion, 1928), p. 11.

13. Francisco de Hollanda, *Four Dialogues on Painting,* trans. Aubrey F.G. Bell (Westport, CN.: Hyperion, 1928), p. 12.

14. Francisco de Hollanda, *Four Dialogues on Painting,* trans. Aubrey F.G. Bell (Westport, CN.: Hyperion, 1928), pp. 15–16.

15. Francisco de Hollanda, *Four Dialogues on Painting,* trans. Aubrey F.G. Bell (Westport, CN.: Hyperion, 1928), p. 15.

16. Francisco de Hollanda, *Four Dialogues on Painting,* trans. Aubrey F.G. Bell (Westport, CN.: Hyperion, 1928), p. 24.

17. Francisco de Hollanda, *Four Dialogues on Painting,* trans. Aubrey F.G. Bell (Westport, CN.: Hyperion, 1928), p. 25.

18. Francisco de Hollanda, *Four Dialogues on Painting,* trans. Aubrey F.G. Bell (Westport, CN.: Hyperion, 1928), p. 25.

19. Francisco de Hollanda, *Four Dialogues on Painting,* trans. Aubrey F.G. Bell (Westport, CN.: Hyperion, 1928), p. 25.

20. Francisco de Hollanda, *Four Dialogues on Painting,* trans. Aubrey F.G. Bell (Westport, CN.: Hyperion, 1928), p. 29.

21. Francisco de Hollanda, *Four Dialogues on Painting,* trans. Aubrey F.G. Bell (Westport, CN.: Hyperion, 1928), p. 31.

22. Francisco de Hollanda, *Four Dialogues on Painting,* trans. Aubrey F.G. Bell (Westport, CN.: Hyperion, 1928), p. 32.

23. Giorgio Vasari, *Vasari on Technique,* trans. Louisa S. Maclehose (New York: Dover, 1960), pp. 205–206.

24. Francisco de Hollanda, *Four Dialogues on Painting,* trans. Aubrey F.G. Bell (Westport, CN.: Hyperion, 1928), pp. 34–35.

25. Francisco de Hollanda, *Four Dialogues on Painting,* trans. Aubrey F.G. Bell (Westport, CN.: Hyperion, 1928), pp. 36–37.

26. Francisco de Hollanda, *Four Dialogues on Painting,* trans. Aubrey F.G. Bell (Westport, CN.: Hyperion, 1928), p. 49.

27. Francisco de Hollanda, *Four Dialogues on Painting,* trans. Aubrey F.G. Bell (Westport, CN.: Hyperion, 1928), p. 50.

28. Francisco de Hollanda, *Four Dialogues on Painting*, trans. Aubrey F.G. Bell (Westport, CN.: Hyperion, 1928), p. 51.

29. Francisco de Hollanda, *Four Dialogues on Painting*, trans. Aubrey F.G. Bell (Westport, CN.: Hyperion, 1928), p. 54.

30. Francisco de Hollanda, *Four Dialogues on Painting*, trans. Aubrey F.G. Bell (Westport, CN.: Hyperion, 1928), p. 55.

31. Francisco de Hollanda, *Four Dialogues on Painting*, trans. Aubrey F.G. Bell (Westport, CN.: Hyperion, 1928), p. 56.

32. Ascanio Condivi, *Life of Michelangelo*, trans. Alice Sedgwick Wohl, ed. Helmut Wohl, Second Edition (University Park: Pennsylvania State University Press, 1976), p. 103.

CHAPTER EIGHT

1. Fabrizio Mancinelli, "The History, Execution Technique, First Censorship and Restoration Intervention," *The Last Judgment: The Restoration*, Vol. 1 (Milan: Rizzoli, 1999), p. 9.

2. Fabrizio Mancinelli, "The History, Execution Technique, First Censorship and Restoration Intervention," *The Last Judgment: The Restoration*, Vol. 1 (Milan: Rizzoli, 1999), p. 11.

3. Loren Partridge, "Michelangelo's Last Judgment: An Interpretation," in Michelangelo, *The Last Judgment: A Glorious Restoration* (New York: Harry N. Abrams, 1997), p. 22.

4. Giorgio Vasari, *The Lives of the Artists*, trans. Julia Conaway Bondanella and Peter Bondanella (Oxford: Oxford University Press, 1998), p. 461.

5. Fabrizio Mancinelli, "The History, Execution Technique, First Censorship and Restoration Intervention," *The Last Judgment: The Restoration*, Vol. 1 (Milan: Rizzoli, 1999), p. 13.

6. Fabrizio Mancinelli, "The History, Execution Technique, First Censorship and Restoration Intervention," *The Last Judgment: The Restoration*, Vol. 1 (Milan: Rizzoli, 1999), p. 13.

7. Valerie Shrimplin, *Sun Symbolism and Cosmology in Michelangelo's Last Judgment* (Kirksville: Truman State University Press, 2000), p. 84.

8. *The Divine Liturgy and the Sunday Gospels* (Hempstead, NY: Ecumenical Publications, 1968), p. 56. The Christmas troparion was written by John of Damascus, who lived from A.D. 646 to 749. It is a standard hymn to be found in the Christmas liturgy of the Greek Orthodox Church.

CHAPTER NINE

1. Alban Butler, *Butler's Lives of the Saints*, Revised Edition (San Francisco: Harper One, 1991).

2. Matthew 16: 19.

3. Matthew 23: 34–40.

4. Fabrizio Mancinelli, "The History, Execution Technique, First Censorship and Restoration Intervention," *The Last Judgment: The Restoration,* Vol. 1 (Milan: Rizzoli, 1999), p. 27.

5. Fabrizio Mancinelli, "The History, Execution Technique, First Censorship and Restoration Intervention," *The Last Judgment: The Restoration,* Vol. 1 (Milan: Rizzoli, 1999), p. 27.

6. Meinolf Schumacher, "Catalogues of Demons as Catalogues of Vices in Medieval German Literature: 'Des Teufels Netz' and the Alexander Romance by Ulrich von Etzenbach," in *The Garden of Evil: The Vices and Culture in the Middle Ages,* ed. Richard Newhauser (Toronto: Pontifical Institute of Mediaeval Studies, 2005), pp. 277–290.

7. Revelations 8: 6.

8. St. Ignatius of Loyola, *Spiritual Exercises,* trans. Eldar Mullan, (S.J., Cosimo Classics, 2007). http://www.cfpeople.org/Books/Exercise/EXERCISEp15.htm

CHAPTER TEN

1. Augustine of Hippo, *City of God,* trans. Henry Bettenson (New York: Penguin Classics, 2003), 22: 20:1. John Dillon and Lloyd P. Gerson, trans. and ed., *Neoplatonic Philosophy. Introductory Readings* (Indianapolis: Hackett Publishing Co., 2004).

2. Valerie Shrimplin, *Sun Symbolism and Cosmology in Michelangelo's Last Judgment* (Kirksville: Truman State University Press, 2000), pp. 265–266.

3. Gianluigi Colalucci, "The Technique and Working Method of Michelangelo in the *Last Judgment,*" *The Last Judgment: The Restoration*, Vol. I (New York: Rizzoli, 1999), p. 84.

4. Subtility: Middle English, from Old French *subtil,* from Latin *subtlis,* fine, delicate; see subtle.

5. Anthony Maas, "General Resurrection," *The Catholic Encyclopedia.* Vol. 12. (New York: Robert Appleton Company, 1911). Accessed December 7, 2008 <http://www.newadvent.org/cathen/12792a.htm>. Joseph Hontheim, "Hell," *The Catholic Encyclopedia.* Vol. 7. (New York: Robert Appleton Company, 1910). Accessed December 7, 2008 <http://www.newadvent.org/cathen/07207a.htm>.

6. Thomas Aquinas and Fathers of the English Dominican Province, *The Summa Theologica of St. Thomas Aquinas* (Five Volumes) (Christian Classics, 1981).

7. John Arendzen, "Docetae." The Catholic Encyclopedia. Vol. 5. New York: Robert Appleton Company, 1909. Accessed December 7, 2008 <http://www.newadvent.org/cathen/05070c.htm>.

CHAPTER ELEVEN

1. Giorgio Vasari, *The Lives of the Artists,* trans. Julia Conaway Bondanella and Peter Bondanella, Oxford: Oxford University Press, 1991, p. 461.

2. Dante Alighieri, *The Divine Comedy, Vol. 1 The Inferno*, Canto 5, lines 4–12. Author's translation.

3. Ascanio Condivi, *The Life of Michelangelo*, trans. Alice Sedgwick Wohl, ed. Hellmut Wohl, Second Edition, University Park: Pennsylvania State University Press, 1999, p. 19.

4. Dante Alighieri, *The Divine Comedy, Vol. 1, The Inferno*, Canto III, Lines 82–93. Author's translation.

5. Giorgio Vasari, *The Lives of the Artists*, trans. Julia Conaway Bondanella and Peter Bondanella, Oxford: Oxford University Press, 1991, p. 462.

6. Giorgio Vasari, *The Lives of the Artists*, trans. Julia Conaway Bondanella and Peter Bondanella, Oxford: Oxford University Press, 1991, p. 462.

CHAPTER TWELVE

1. Ascanio Condivi, *Life of Michelangelo*, trans. Alice Sedgwick Wohl, ed. Helmut Wohl, Second Edition (University Park: Pennsylvania State University Press, 1976), p. 87.

2. Giorgio Vasari, "Life of Michelangelo" (1550), in *Michelangelo, Poems and Letters*, trans. Anthony Mortimer (London: Penguin Books, 2007), p. 179.

3. I use "Counter-Reformation" and "Catholic Reformation" interchangeably, since they both refer to the same period and to the same movement within the Catholic Church.

4. Matthew 16: 19.

5. George Bull, *Michelangelo: A Biography* (New York: St. Martins, 1995), p. 296.

6. Anthony Hughes, *Michelangelo*, Art and Ideas series (London: Phaidon, 1997), p. 283.

7. George Bull, *Michelangelo: A Biography* (New York: St. Martins, 1995), p. 295.

8. Pietro Aretino, *Lettere e Scritte a Pietro Aretino* (Roma: Salerno, 2003–), LXXXIII, p. 916.

9. Bernardine Barnes, *Michelangelo's Last Judgment: A Renaissance Response* (Berkeley: University of California Press, 1998), p. 84.

10. Timothy Hampton, *Writing from History: The Rhetoric of Exemplarity in Renaissance Literature* (Syracuse: Cornell University Press, 1990), p. 119.

11. John Addington Symonds, *The Life of Michelangelo Buonarroti* (Bibliobazaar, 2006), pp. 300–301.

CHAPTER THIRTEEN

1. George Bull, *Michelangelo: A Biography* (New York: St. Martin's Griffin, 1995), pp. 394–395.

2. Michelangelo, *Rime,* introduzione di Giovanni Testori, cronologia, promessa e note a cura di Ettore Barelli (Milano: Biblioteca Universale Rizzoli, 1975), no. 247, p. 281.

3. Michelangelo Buonarroti, *Il carteggio di Michelangelo,* edizione postuma di Giovanni Poggi, a cura di Paola Barocchi e Renzo Ristori (Firenze: Sansoni, 1965), Vol. V, MCCCXCI, MCCCXCII.

4. Michelangelo Buonarroti, *Il carteggio di Michelangelo,* edizione postuma di Giovanni Poggi, a cura di Paola Barocchi e Renzo Ristori (Firenze: Sansoni, 1965), Vol. V, MCCCXCII.

5. George Bull, *Michelangelo: A Biography* (New York: St. Martin's Griffin, 1995), p. 416.

INDEX